HOTSPOTS
MALLORCA

Written by Tony Kelly; updated by Teresa Fisher and Mary-Ann Gallagher

Published by Thomas Cook Publishing
A division of Thomas Cook Tour Operations Limited
Company registration no. 1450464 England
The Thomas Cook Business Park, Unit 9, Coningsby Road,
Peterborough PE3 8SB, United Kingdom
Email: sales@thomascook.com, Tel: +44 (0) 1733 416477
www.thomascookpublishing.com

Produced by Cambridge Publishing Management Limited
Burr Elm Court, Main Street, Caldecote CB23 7NU

ISBN: 978-1-84157-913-9

First edition © 2006 Thomas Cook Publishing
Text © 2008 Thomas Cook Publishing
Maps © 2008 Thomas Cook Publishing

Series Editor: Diane Ashmore
Production/DTP: Steven Collins

Printed and bound in Spain by GraphyCems

Cover photography © SIME/Damm Fridmar

CONTENTS

WHAT'S IN YOUR GUIDEBOOK?

Independent authors Impartial up-to-date information from our travel experts who meticulously source local knowledge.

Experience Thomas Cook's 165 years in the travel industry and guidebook publishing enriches every word with expertise you can trust.

Travel know-how Contributions by thousands of staff around the globe, each one living and breathing travel.

Editors Travel-publishing professionals, pulling everything together to craft a perfect blend of words, pictures, maps and design.

You, the traveller We deliver a practical, no-nonsense approach to information, geared to how you really use it.

● *C̀ɑp de Formentor, north Mallorca*

INTRODUCTION
Getting to know Mallorca

Mallorca

0 — 8 km
0 — 4 miles

○ City
○ Large Town
○ Small Town
■ POI
▬ Motorway
— Main Road
— Minor Road
✈ Airport
╫ Railway

Puig de Massanella ▲ 1345

Port de Sóller (Ma-10)

Sóller (Ma-10)

Punta de Deià (Ma-10)

Deià

Valldemossa (Ma-11)

Lloseta

Banyalbufar (Ma-10)

Bunyola

Binissalem

Santa Maria del Camí (Ma-13)

Esporles

Serra de Tramuntana

Puig de Galatzó ▲ 1026

Puigpunyent

Festival Park

Marratxí

Sa Dragonera (Ma-10)

Sant Elm

Andratx

Calvià (Ma-20)

PALMA

Port d'Andratx

Peguera

Illetes

Camp (Ma-1c) de Mar

Fundació Pilar i Joan Miró (Ma-19)

C'an Partilla & Playa de Palma

Cap des Llamp

Torrenova

Palma Nova

S'Arenal

Son Sant Joan ✈

Santa Ponça

Magaluf

(Ma-19)

El Toro

Palma Bay

Cap de Cala Figuera

Vallgornera

Cap Blanc

France

Spain

Mallorca

Algeria

Getting to know Mallorca

Mallorca is Europe's favourite holiday destination – and it is easy to see why. A warm climate guarantees sunshine throughout the summer, when the temperatures rise well over 30 °C (86 °F). Its beaches of pale gold sand are perfect for swimming and sunbathing, while the calm, clear waters and sheltered bays make excellent conditions for watersports. You can eat well with choices ranging from plain grilled fish, straight off the fishing boat, to the finest international cuisine, and the nightlife is some of the hottest in Europe – though if it is peace and quiet you are after, that shouldn't be too hard to find either.

ISLAND OF CONTRASTS

Each of the regions of Mallorca has its own distinct character. The south coast, around the capital, Palma de Mallorca, is where you will find the liveliest resorts as well as some of the island's best beaches – many of which have been awarded the European Union's Blue Flag for their cleanliness and facilities. The north and west coastlines, by contrast, form a region of wild and rugged beauty, dominated by the Serra de Tramuntana mountain range which runs the length of the coast. The northeast, around Alcúdia, has some of Mallorca's oldest historical monuments as well as two of the island's longest beaches, while, further south, the east coast is studded with tiny *cales*, or pine-fringed coves. At the centre of it all is Es Pla, a fertile plain of almond and apricot groves dotted with solid market towns where life goes on as it always has, as if tourism had never been discovered. And don't forget Palma itself, which is one of the most stylish and cosmopolitan cities in Europe.

SOMETHING FOR EVERYONE

Mallorca has something for everybody; whatever you want from your holiday, you will probably find it here. Children will love the beaches, the water parks and the magic of the sea, and adults can relax knowing that the kids are having fun, while those who like nothing better than lying on a beach, soaking up the sun, will definitely be spoilt for choice.

◔ *A terrace café in the pretty village of Sóller*

THE BEST OF MALLORCA

TOP 10 ATTRACTIONS

PALMA DE MALLORCA

- **Banys Arabs (Arab Baths)** Dating from the 9th century, these elegant baths survive from Mallorca's long period of Moorish occupation (see page 15).

- **Castell de Bellver (Bellver Castle)** This 14th-century castle on top of a steep hill in Palma now houses the Palma History Museum and is surrounded by a park (see page 15).

- **Cathedral, Almudaina Palace and surrounding areas** The magnificent Gothic cathedral dominates the old quarter of Palma (see page 17). The interior is richly decorated with works of religious art, illuminated by a stained-glass rose window. The Almudaina Palace, next to it, originally the residence of the Moorish kings of Mallorca, is now the official Palma residence of the Spanish king and queen.

- **Mountain train and tram** Take the old wooden train from Palma over the Serra de Tramuntana mountains to Sóller (see page 86). Spectacular views are guaranteed. Then board a historic tram for the final leg of the journey to Port de Sóller (see page 82).

- **Deià** An 'artists' village', where the English writer Robert Graves lived until his death in 1985. His home, Ca N'Alluny, is now a fascinating museum (see page 79).

- **Valldemossa** Another attractive old village. Chopin, the Polish composer, spent a winter at the Charterhouse monastery here in 1838–9 and composed several works (see page 75).

- **S'Albufera Natural Park** A wetlands area and wildlife reserve, and an important breeding and staging post for more than 200 species of birds (see page 48).

- **Artà** A beautiful inland town with a remarkable medieval atmosphere. The hilltop Sanctuary of Sant Salvador lies within the walls of the old Moorish citadel (see page 50).

CALA D'OR
- **Cala Figuera** One of the prettiest fishing villages in Mallorca. The fishermen's houses line the banks of the narrow cala, or bay, on which the village stands, and each one has a boathouse built beside it (see page 66).

PORTOCRISTO
- **Coves del Drac (Dragon Caves)** The most spectacular underground caverns in Mallorca, containing one of the biggest underground lakes in the world (see page 58). The nearby Coves dels Hams are not as big but are still impressive (see page 58).

▼ *Olive grove near Palma de Mallorca*

SYMBOLS KEY

The following is a key to the symbols used throughout this book:

ⓐ address **ⓣ** telephone **ⓦ** website address **ⓔ** email **ⓛ** opening times
ⓝ public transport connections **ⓘ** important

ⓘ	information office	**O**	city
✉	post office	**O**	large town
🛍	shopping	**○**	small town
✈	airport	**■**	poi (point of interest)
✚	hospital	**═**	motorway
🛡	police station	**—**	main road
🚌	bus station/stop	**—**	minor road
🚆	railway station	**—**	railway
✝	church		
❶	numbers denote featured cafés, restaurants & evening venues		

RESTAURANT CATEGORIES

Meals are rated according to the following guidelines. Please note, each rating is based on the cost of a main course for one person without drinks.

£ = under €15 **££** = €15–€30 **£££** = over €30

ⓓ *Mallorca attracts many pleasure crafts to its harbours*

RESORTS
Places under the sun

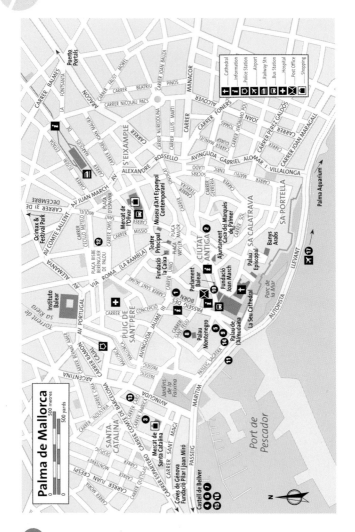

Palma de Mallorca

Cathedral	Police Station	Hospital
Information	Airport	Shopping
	Railway Stn	
	Bus Station	
	Post Office	

Puerto Portals

Palma Aquarium

Octimax & Festival Park

Instituto Balear

Mercat de l'Olivar

Museu d'Art Espanyol Contemporani

Teatre Principal

Fundació la Caixa

Parlament Balear

Fundació Joan March

Ciutat Antiga

Ajuntament

Casa del Marqués de Palmer

Palau Episcopal

Banys Àrabs

Sa Calatrava

Sa Portella

La Seu Cathedral

Port de la Mar

Passeig des Born

Palau Montenegro

Palau de l'Almudaina

Puig de Sant Pere

Santa Catalina

Mercat de Santa Catalina

Fundació Pilar i Joan Miró

Coves de Gènova

Castell de Bellver

Port de Pescador

Jardins de sa Faixina

0   500 metres
0   500 yards

N

Palma de Mallorca (Palma Town)

Palma de Mallorca, beautifully situated at the centre of Palma Bay, is the capital of the Balearic Islands. This vibrant, cosmopolitan city has managed to retain a great deal of its ancient charm. Its bustling street life and thriving arts scene lead many people to compare it with the stylish Catalan capital, Barcelona, and it was recently chosen by a leading Spanish newspaper as the best place to live in Spain.

The most striking image of Palma is its cathedral, standing proud on the waterfront and seeming almost to grow out of the sea. Behind the cathedral is the old Arab quarter, a warren of narrow lanes shielding ancient palaces and mansions, with elegant courtyards featuring stone stairways and potted plants. A short stroll from here leads to **Plaça Major**, a pleasant square of open-air cafés, at the heart of the pedestrian shopping district with its many small speciality shops. Amble down **La Rambla**, with its dozens of flower-sellers, and the tree-lined **Passeig des Born**, to return to the waterfront where the real lifeblood of Palma lies. Fishermen mend their nets, cruise ships drift into the harbour, and the designer bars along the **Passeig Marítim** buzz with conversation after dark.

THINGS TO SEE & DO

Banys Arabs (Arab Baths)
The ornate columns and elegant domes of these baths, dating from the 10th century, are one of the few surviving monuments from Mallorca's long period of Moorish rule.
ⓐ Carrer Serra 7 ❶ 971 72 15 49 ❺ 09.00–20.00 (summer); 09.00–17.45 (winter) ❶ Admission charge

Castell de Bellver (Bellver Castle)
This circular castle, high in the woods above Palma Bay, was built in the 14th century soon after the Catalan conquest. It also houses the Palma History Museum and the Despuig sculpture collection.

a Parc Bellver (take a taxi from Palma, or bus no 3 and walk)
☎ 971 73 06 57 **🕐** 08.00–20.00 Mon–Sat, 10.00–17.00 Sun (Oct–Mar);
08.00–21.30 Mon–Sat, 10.00–19.00 Sun (Apr–Sept); museums closed Sun
❶ Admission charge

City sightseeing hop on / hop off bus
This bus takes tourists to all the major attractions. It has 16 stops and
tickets are valid for 24 hours. **🅦** www.citysightseeing-spain.com

Fundació La Caixa (CaixaForum)
This art gallery in the former Gran Hotel has a permanent exhibition of
Mallorcan paintings as well as changing temporary displays. The ground-
floor café is one of Palma's smartest meeting-spots, and the building itself,
a fine example of Catalan Modernist architecture, is also worth a look.
a Plaça Weyler 3 **☎** 971 17 85 00 **🕐** 10.00–21.00 Mon–Sat,
10.00–14.00 Sun **❶** Free admission

Fundació Joan March (Joan March Gallery)
This small but dazzling display of contemporary Spanish art includes
some treasures by Picasso, Salvador Dalí and Miró.

> ## SHOPPING
> Serious shoppers should head for **Avinguda Jaume III**, where most of
> the city's boutiques are situated. Here you can find leather goods,
> designer clothes, jewellery and antiques as well as a branch of Spain's
> top department store, **El Corte Inglés**. Those who enjoy browsing in
> small, specialist shops should make for the area around **Plaça Major**.
>
> **Markets**: Palma's main market is held six mornings a week (not
> Sundays) in the Olivar market hall near **Plaça d'Espanya**. A *baratillo*
> (flea market) takes place each Saturday morning on the ring road
> at **Avinguda Gabriel Alomar i Villalonga**. There is also a lively
> open-air craft market during the week in the Plaça Major.

ⓐ Carrer de Sant Miquel II ⓣ 971 71 35 15
ⓦ www.march.es/arte/ingles/palma ⓛ 10.00–18.30 Mon–Fri,
10.00–14.00 Sat ⓘ Free admission

Passeig Marítim
Starting near the cathedral, stroll the length of this seafront promenade past the small traditional fishing port (the Port de Pesca) and the seemingly endless rows of luxury yachts and motorboats to the Estació Marítimo (the ship terminal) at the far end, where naval ships, cruise liners and ferries from mainland Spain dock, and you will soon appreciate Palma's long-standing love affair with the sea. Plenty of bars and restaurants for refreshments as you go.

La Rambla
La Rambla has been one of the city's main promenades for years. This tree-lined avenue is filled with the stalls of Palma's daily flower market.

La Seu Cathedral
Palma's marvellous Gothic cathedral occupies a prominent position overlooking the sea at the edge of the old city. It was begun in the 13th century but has been extensively remodelled over the years, most recently by the famous Catalan architect Antoni Gaudí at the start of the 20th century. Recently, internationally famous Mallorcan artist Miquel Barceló has created a magnificent, but controversial, new chapel.
ⓐ Plaça Almoina s/n ⓛ 10.00–17.15 Mon–Fri (Apr, May, Oct); 10.00–18.15 (June–Sept); 10.00–15.15 (Nov–Mar); 10.00–14.15 Sat; closed Sun except for High Mass at 10.30, 12.00, 13.00 and 19.00 ⓘ Admission charge

The *Majorca Daily Bulletin*, a newspaper published in English six times a week, is a Palma institution. You can buy it at newsstands all over the city, or pick up a copy at one of the tourist offices.

🔺 *La Seu, Palma's cathedral*

EXCURSIONS

Coves de Génova (Caves of Génova)
These interesting caves can be found in the charming village of Gènova, high on the slopes of the Serra de Na Burguesa hills above Palma.
ⓐ Carrer de Barranc 45 (easily reached by bus no 4) ☎ 971 40 23 87
🕐 10.00–13.30 & 16.00–19.00 (summer); 10.30–13.00 & 16.00–18.00 (winter) ❶ Admission charge

Festival Park
This spacious leisure complex has an enormous range of facilities and activities on offer. There are 29 different shops and factory outlets, 30 restaurants, including Chinese, Greek and Italian, two cinemas and 22-lane bowling. Enjoy evening open-air entertainment in the centre square or visit the summer crafts market.
ⓐ Palma – Inca road just before Santa Maria (train from Plaça Espanya, Palma to Marratxi, then a five-minute walk) 🌐 www.festivalparks.com
🕐 Shops 10.00–22.00; park open until early hours; summer market 18.00–23.00 Fri–Sat

Fundació Pilar i Joan Miró (Pilar and Juan Miró Gallery)

The abstract Catalan artist Joan Miró lived on Mallorca for much of his life, and his house and studio have been turned into a museum of his work. The studio itself has been left largely untouched since his death in 1983, with tins of paint still lying around open on the tables.

ⓐ Carrer Joan de Saridakis 29, Cala Major (taxi or buses no 3, 4, 21 from Palma) ☎ 971 70 14 20 ⓦ http://miro.palmademallorca.es ⏰ 10.00–19.00 (summer); 10.00–18.00 Tues–Sat, 10.00–15.00 Sun (winter); closed Mon ❶ Admission charge

Ocimax

The leisure centre in Palma has 15 cinema screens and 26-lane bowling. Wide choice of restaurants and bars. Gymnasium and children's play park. Ample parking.

ⓐ Carrer Leocadia Togorens (opposite Carrefour Hypermarket) ☎ 971 49 87 53

Puerto Portals

The St Tropez of the Balearics and Mallorca's most glamorous resort. Its glitzy marina, crammed with fashionable restaurants and bars, is a great venue for people-watching and celebrity-spotting.

TAKING A BREAK

Restaurants & bars

Bar Bosch £ ❶ This café-bar at the top of the Passeig des Born has long been one of the city's most popular meeting places. ⓐ Plaça Rei Joan Carles I ☎ 971 72 11 31 ⏰ 08.00–02.00

Ca'n Joan de S'Aigo £ ❷ Pastries, cakes, almond ice cream and scrumptious hot chocolate are on the menu at this 200-year-old café. ⓐ Carrer Ca'n Sanc 10 ☎ 971 71 07 59 ⏰ 08.00–21.00

Sa Llimona £ ❸ This is the place to try Mallorca's best-known snack, *pa amb oli*, which is country bread rubbed with tomato and a hint of garlic,

then drizzled with olive oil. ⓐ Carrer Fàbrica 27 ① 971 73 50 96 &
ⓐ Carrer Sant Magí 80 ① 971 28 00 23 ◔ 20.00–24.00

Mesón C'An Pedro I and II £ ④ You'll find typical Mallorcan specialities
at both outposts of this long-established tavern along with a few veggie
options. It is a great choice for families. ⓐ Carrer Rector Vives 4 & 14
① 971 70 21 62 ◔ 12.30–16.30 & 19.00–00.30 Thur–Tues

Abaco ££ ⑤ Unusual cocktail bar inside a 17th-century palace, with
caged birds, fountains and classical music. ⓐ Carrer Sant Joan 1
① 971 71 49 39 ◔ 20.00–01.30 Sun–Thur, 20.00–03.30 Fri & Sat

Arrocería Sa Cranca ££ ⑥ The speciality at this restaurant on the seafront
is paella. ⓐ Passeig Marítim 13 ① 971 73 74 47 ◔ 13.00–15.45 &
20.00–23.30 Tues–Sat, 13.00–15.45 Sun

Baisakhi ££ ⑦ This high-class Indian restaurant on the waterfront has
developed an excellent reputation over the years. New menu chosen by
the owner every day. ⓐ Passeig Marítim 8 ① 971 73 68 06
◔ Two sittings: 20.00 & 23.00 Tues–Sun

Bon Lloc ££ ⑧ This vegetarian restaurant is popular for its good-value
lunchtime set menu. ⓐ Carrer Sant Feliu 7 ① 971 71 86 17
◔ 13.00–16.00 Tues–Sat

La Bóveda ££ ⑨ This is definitely the best and most popular tapas bar
in Palma. Choose from *pa amb oli*, cured ham, mussels and octopus,
which you eat standing. ⓐ Carrer Botería 3 ① 971 71 48 63
◔ 13.30–16.00 & 20.30–24.00 Mon–Sat

Es Parlement ££ ⑩ Located in the Balearic Parliament buildings, this
traditional restaurant reputedly serves the best *paella ciega* ('blind
paella' – without the bones) in town. ⓐ Carrer de Conquistador 11
① 971 72 60 26 ◔ 13.00–16.00 & 20.00–23.00 Mon–Sat

Port Pesquer ££ ⑪ This place is perfectly located on Palma's waterfront. A chic café with live music on Thursdays and Fridays, it serves great tapas. ⓐ Passeig Marítim, near the fishing port ⓣ 971 71 52 20 ⓛ 09.00–03.00

Sa Premsa ££ ⑫ This is a typical Mallorcan cellar-restaurant, in a converted garage with wine vats around the walls. The food is rustic, with dishes such as *frit mallorquí* (see page 94) and pork wrapped in cabbage leaves. ⓐ Plaça Bisbe Berenguer de Palou 8 ⓣ 971 72 35 29 ⓛ 12.30–16.00 & 19.30–23.30 Mon–Sat

Wasabi ££ ⑬ This trendy Japanese fusion restaurant and sushi bar attracts hip young locals as well as tourists. ⓐ Carrer Caro 16 ⓣ 971 45 65 93 ⓛ 13.30–15.30 & 20.00–23.30 Tues–Sun

Caballito de Mar £££ ⑭ Fresh fish and seafood dishes are the specialities at this busy seafront restaurant. ⓐ Passeig Sagrera 5 ⓣ 971 72 10 74 ⓛ 13.00–16.00 & 20.00–24.00; closed Mon (winter)

AFTER DARK

Bars & clubs
Most of the late-night action in Palma takes place along the Passeig Marítim. A younger crowd heads for **Abraxas** ⑮ formerly Pacha, with a fabulous garden terrace (ⓛ 23.00–06.00), while a slightly older crowd gathers at **Tito's** ⑯ Palma's largest nightclub, with six bars, a laser show and great views over the bay (ⓐ Use the outdoor lifts from Passeig Marítim ⓦ www.titosmallorca.com ⓛ 22.00–06.00).

Son Amar ⑰ Mallorca's top nightspot lies just outside Palma, in a converted 16th-century mansion on the road to Sóller. The cabaret show here features flamenco and Spanish ballet, flying dancers and a live concert by a cover band. ⓐ Carretera de Sóller, Km 10, Bunyola ⓣ 900 71 23 45 ⓦ www.sonamar.com

Illetes

Illetes takes its name from the pair of rocky islets that can be seen just offshore. This relatively low-key resort is a Spanish residential area and also a popular weekend outing for families from Palma, with the result that it is by far the most Spanish of the Bay of Palma resorts.

BEACHES

The main beach, **Platja d'Illetes**, is right in the centre of the resort and has plenty of sunbeds and parasols for hire as well as several snack bars right beside the sea. A short walk leads past the tiny **Platja Cala Comptessa** to **Platja d'Illetes III**, which is quieter and has fewer facilities.

TAKING A BREAK

Restaurants & bars
Stroll along to the resort of Sant Agustí for a wealth of choice. Excellent French, Chinese and Indian restaurants, and even a Russian one.

Calypso £ Very friendly family-run bar-cafeteria. Children's menu available. ⓐ Passeig Illetes 22 🕐 10.00 until late Tues–Sun

Mooncala £ This trendy but laid-back beach bar offers reasonably priced home cooking. ⓐ Avinguda Joan Miró 305, Sant Agustí ☎ 971 40 43 10 🕐 12.00–01.00

The Rose Mallow £ This olde-worlde English pub has lots of character, friendly staff, and afternoon cream teas with homemade cakes and

> Trying to find a parking space in Illetes can be a nightmare. It is much easier to use the regular bus service from Palma.

⬤ *Beach at Illetes*

scones. ⓐ Passeig Illetes 4 ☏ 971 40 18 81 🕒 11.00 until late, closed Sun (winter)

Illetes Playa ££ An excellent Mallorcan restaurant with an international flavour and a generally upmarket, formal approach. ⓐ Passeig Illetes 75 (Centro comercial) ☏ 971 70 18 96 🕒 13.00–16.30 & 19.00–23.00

Es Parral ££ Chicken Mallorcan style is the speciality. ⓐ Passeig Illetes 75 (Centro comercial) ☏ 971 70 11 27 🕒 12.30–16.00 & 18.00–24.00

AFTER DARK

Clubs
Virtual Club A spectacular bar, set in natural caves beside the sea, attached to a smart restaurant and beach club. ⓐ Passeig Illetes 60 ☏ 971 70 32 35 ⓦ www.virtualclub.es 🕒 12.00–02.00

Palma Nova

Sandwiched between the ritzy harbour at Puerto Portals and the riotous nightlife of Magaluf, Palma Nova is an excellent resort for families, with a wide, sandy bay of golden beaches and two of Mallorca's leading family attractions.

BEACHES

The main beach at Palma Nova is divided into two sections, both well equipped with sunbeds, showers, lifeguards and warning flags. A third beach, Son Maties, lies just around the bay.

THINGS TO SEE & DO

Golf Fantasia
Of all the mini-golf courses in Mallorca, this one, set amid waterfalls, caves and tropical gardens, is one of the best. There is a choice of three different courses – or you can stay all day and play all 54 holes.
ⓐ Carrer Tenis 3 ☎ 971 13 50 40 🕐 10.00–02.00 🌐 www.golffantasia.com
❶ Admission charge

⬥ *A dolphin show at Marineland*

Marineland

Performing dolphins, sea lions and parrots are the star turns at this sea-life centre. There is also a penguin pool, a reptile house and an aquarium with sharks and tropical fish on display.

ⓐ Carretera Palma–Andratx ⓣ 971 67 51 25 ⓦ www.marineland.es
ⓛ Mid-Mar to Nov; dolphin shows 11.45, 15.45, 17.45; parrot shows 10.30, 13.00, 16.30; sea lion shows 11.30, 15.30, 17.30 ⓘ Admission charge

TAKING A BREAK

Restaurants

Ciro's ££ Dine on the terrace overlooking the sea at this long-established restaurant, which offers a wide variety of Mediterranean specialities from paella to *caldereta* (lobster stew). For afternoon tea, try the adjoining *salon de té*. ⓐ Passeig del Mar 3 ⓣ 971 68 10 52
ⓛ 12.30–24.00

La Cucaracha ££ Palma Nova's only Mexican restaurant, serving fajitas, nachos and other Mexican specialities. ⓐ Passeig del Mar 20
ⓣ 971 68 30 45 ⓛ 18.30–24.00

Real Dion ££ A top-quality British-run restaurant serving imaginative home-cooked food. The house speciality is roast lamb, but the more adventurous can try salmon in champagne sauce followed by raspberry brûlée. ⓐ Passeig del Mar 16 ⓣ 971 68 24 57 ⓛ 19.00–24.00 (summer); Thur–Sun only (winter)

AFTER DARK

Bars

Pub Papis Wide variety of music and themed nights which are very popular with the young crowd. ⓐ Carrer Pedro Vaquer 2 ⓣ 971 68 30 96
ⓛ 06.00–04.00 ⓘ Admission free

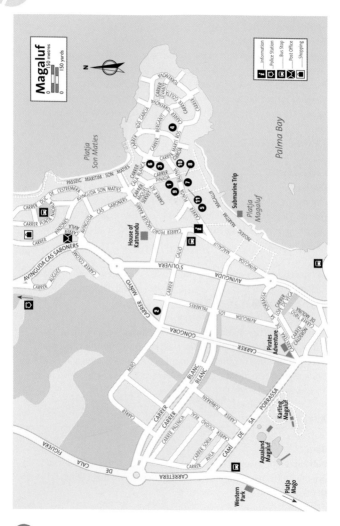

Magaluf

What was once no more than a quiet fishing village surrounded by marshes on the edge of Palma Bay has been transformed over the last 40 years into a pulsating mega-resort. The beach is one of the best on the island and there are canoes and pedal boats for hire, as well as windsurfing and snorkelling equipment. But most visitors to Magaluf save their energy for the legendary round-the-clock nightlife.

BEACHES

Magaluf's beach runs parallel to the main street of the resort. Within walking distance is **Platja Son Maties**, on the edge of Palma Nova (see map opposite). Portals Vells, on the headland south of Magaluf, has two small beaches including **Platja Mago**, one of Mallorca's official nudist beaches.

THINGS TO SEE & DO

Aqualand Magaluf
A giant water park with death-defying slides, thrilling rides for older kids and some tamer ones for the toddlers. Next door is **Western Park**.
ⓐ Carretera de Cala Figuera, on the edge of Magaluf ❶ 971 13 08 11 (Aqualand); 971 13 12 03 (Western Park) ⓦ www.aqualand.es; www.westernpark.com/magaluf/mallorca ❶ 10.00–18.00 (July–Aug); 10.00–17.00 (May–June & Sept–Oct); closed Nov–Apr ❶ Admission charge

House of Katmandu
Magaluf's newest attraction is a fantastical Tibetan-style mansion which is lodged upside-down in the ground. In this exciting audio-visual adventure, visitors discover the Chamber of Pain and the Cave of Shivers and come face to face with a yeti.
ⓐ Carrer Pedro Vaquer Ramis s/n ❶ 971 13 46 60
ⓦ www.houseofkatmandu.com ❶ 10.00–01.00 ❶ Admission charge

Karting Magaluf

Older children will enjoy racing around the **Karting Magaluf** track.
ⓐ Camí de Sa Porrassa (next to Aquapark) ❶ 971 13 17 34
ⓦ www.kartingmagaluf.com ❷ 10.00–24.00 (July–Aug); 10.00–sunset
(Sept–June)

Pirates Adventure

A great family outing with a swashbuckling pirates adventure show.
Audience participation is encouraged. Booking advised.
ⓐ Carretera de sa Porrassa ❶ 971 13 04 11 ⓦ www.piratesadventure.com
❷ May–Nov; family show 15.00, 18.00, 20.00; adult show 21.00, 23.00
(times may vary)

Submarine trips

A 50-minute underwater excursion in a genuine submarine is the highlight of the **Nemo Submarine** two-hour trip from Magaluf
(ⓐ Carrer Galió 2 ❶ 971 13 02 44 ❷ 09.00–20.00; closed Nov
❶ Children under 3 not allowed). **Neptuno-Sub** is a cruise around the
southwest coast on a triple-deck catamaran with underwater viewing
windows (❶ 971 13 12 11 for reservations).

TAKING A BREAK

Restaurants & bars

Eastenders £ ❶ 'Just like home' is the promise of this very English
restaurant, where roast beef and Yorkshire pudding take top billing.
ⓐ Carrer Pinada 6 ❶ 971 68 26 17 ❷ 09.00–03.30

Mrs Doyle's £ ❷ Irish pub food all day and buzzing in the evening with
a fiddler and other entertainment, followed by a disco. Very friendly.
ⓐ Carrer Galió 51 ❷ 10.00–02.00 Mar–Oct

Pacha's Pub £ ❸ One of the best-known cocktail bars in Magaluf.
ⓐ Carrer Martí Ros García 12 ❷ 12.00–04.00

Los Caracoles ££ ❹ A traditional Spanish restaurant known for its excellent steaks. ⓐ Galerías Joboso, Carrer Martí Ros García ⓣ 971 68 02 67 ⓛ 12.30–16.00 & 19.00–24.00 Tues–Sun

Pirates Beach Bar & Grill ££ ❺ The enormously successful Pirates Adventure has just opened a new beach bar and grill in a 'shipwreck'. ⓐ Carrer Punta Ballena ⓣ 971 13 04 11 ⓛ 10.00–14.00

El Salmon ££ ❻ This restaurant is known for its well-presented Mallorcan and international cuisine. The atmosphere is elegant but relaxed. ⓐ Carrer Cala Blanca 10 ⓣ 971 68 00 10 ⓛ 12.00–14.00 & 18.00–01.00 Mon–Sat; 18.00–01.00 Sun

AFTER DARK

Bars & clubs
Channis ❼ and **Bar 29** ❽ (opposite BCM) are popular pre-club bars to start off the night. **BCM** ❾ spreads over 3 floors and top international DJs come here to do their thing. The most spectacular lighting systems in Europe are on the upper level. Smart but casual dress. Age range 16–30. ⓐ All can be found at Avinguda S'Olivera 2

Fusion ❿ All-night disco with pop and chart sounds. ⓐ Carrer Punta Balena 24

Tokio Joe's ⓫ House and garage music with six large bars. ⓐ Carrer Punta Balena 7 ⓣ 971 13 01 85

> ## MAGALUF CLUB PASS
> This pass gives visitors entrance to five of the best-known clubs in town for one special price. It is available at Bananas, Boomerangs, Tokio Joe's, Legends and Honeys. More information at ⓦ www.magallufclubpass.com

Torrenova

The Torrenova area is a fun-orientated district of Magaluf with lots of things to see and do right around the clock, so it's suitable for young people and families alike. Dance the night away in the district's many discos and bars, or just relax and chill out in its quieter outskirts.

THINGS TO SEE & DO

Boat trips
Numerous boat excursions can be taken around the area's bays, providing glimpses of the local marine life that Mallorca has to offer.

Cycling
Hire a bike for an hour or a day. **Pepe** has tandems, tricycles and even family-sized 'safari' bikes.
ⓐ Carrer Cala Blanca ⓣ 971 68 03 14 ⓛ 08.00–22.00

Watersports
Torrenova offers an extensive selection of watersports. You can experience the breeze in your hair while on skis, or relax underwater while diving to the shallow depths of the warm and calm waters.

TAKING A BREAK

Restaurants & bars
The Blue Bar £ A classic seafront restaurant and bar, this serves everything from a full English breakfast to typical Spanish specialities.
ⓐ Carrer Martí Ros García 6 ⓣ 971 68 30 04 ⓛ 09.00–02.00; closed Mon & Tues (winter)

The Prince William £ A large pub, popular with British visitors to the resort. ⓐ Carrer Pinada 1 ⓛ 11.00–05.00

Robin Hood £ Friendly local restaurant serving home-cooked British food. Extensive menu served with a friendly smile. Great breakfasts! ⓐ Carrer Sant Miquel de Liria 10 ⓣ 971 68 34 37 ⓛ 09.00–23.00 (May–Oct)

Nawaab Indian Restaurant ££ Find all your favourite Indian dishes as mild or hot as you like. Take-aways too. ⓐ Carrer Almirante Ferraont 2 ⓣ 971 13 09 34 ⓛ 12.00–01.00

Ruby Tuesdays ££ Dinner, including children's meals, with karaoke and other pub fun. Chill out on the terrace bar with the spectacular views over Palma Nova and Palma Bay. ⓐ Carrer Martí Ros García 6 ⓣ 971 68 33 63 ⓛ 10.00–02.00 (summer); closed winter

AFTER DARK

Clubs

Banana Techno/house/garage music. Mermaids swim in a glass pool. ⓐ Carrer Martí Ros García 2 ⓛ 22.30–06.00 ⓘ Admission charge

Carwash The dancing staff wear 1970s clothes but the music ranges from 1970s and 1980s to the latest sounds. Casual dress. ⓐ Garci de Ruiz 11 ⓣ 971 68 34 07 ⓛ 22.00–06.00 ⓘ Admission charge

Poco Loco Great party atmosphere, resident British DJ and commercial dance music. ⓐ Carrer Martí Ros García 5 ⓛ 22.00–06.00

SHOPPING

Marina Shopping Centre Offering restaurants, boutiques, perfume, jewellery and sports shops, all at tax-free prices.
Punta Balena main strip Local products, souvenir shops, jewellers, shoe shops, boutiques, supermarkets, perfumeries – anything you want is along this main strip.

Santa Ponça

Santa Ponça is a lively resort on the southwest coast, built around a marina and an excellent beach. The town has an important place in Mallorcan history, as it is here that Jaume I began his successful campaign to drive the Moors from the island in 1929. It was this invasion that paved the way for Mallorca to become a part of modern Spain.

BEACHES

The main beach, a horseshoe of golden sand, lies close to the centre of the resort and offers a variety of watersports. A smaller beach, set in its own sheltered cove, can be reached from Avinguda Rei Jaume I, about a 15-minute walk from the main beach. From here it is a short stroll to the Creu de la Conquesta (Conquest Cross), with panoramic views over the bay.

THINGS TO SEE & DO

Golf
Golf Santa Ponça has been home to the Balearic Open and includes two 18-hole courses and one 9-hole course.
ⓐ Urbanización Santa Ponça, Palma-Andratx Road, Km 18, just outside the resort ⓣ 971 69 02 11 ⓛ All year

Scuba diving
If you want to try your hand at scuba diving, **Centro de Buceo Zoea** offers equipment hire and tuition.
ⓐ Club Náutico Santa Ponça ⓣ 971 69 14 44 ⓦ www.zoeamallorca.com

TAKING A BREAK

Restaurants & bars
Durty Nelly's £ Along with its sister pub, Sean's Place, it promises

great craic! Resident band 'The Weightless Astronauts' entertains you with traditional and contemporary music. ⓐ Carrer Ramon Montcada ⓑ 12.00–01.00

Simsalabim £ Sample pizzas in an incredible setting decorated to resemble a nomad's tent from the Arabian Nights. ⓐ Avinguda Jaume I 111 ⓣ 971 69 78 04 ⓑ 12.00–24.00

Mesón del Rey ££ A typically Spanish restaurant in a quiet backstreet. The paella is particularly good. ⓐ Carrer Puig des Teix 15 ⓣ 971 69 08 15 ⓑ 13.00–16.00 & 19.00–24.00; closed Nov

Restaurante Oeste ££ The ultimate dining experience with such delicacies as kangaroo, ostrich and wild boar but also traditional dishes. ⓐ Avinguda Jaume I 84 ⓣ 971 69 02 66 ⓑ 18.30–24.00 (Oct–Mar/Apr); closed winter

AFTER DARK

Clubs
Fama This nightclub is particularly popular at weekends. Spanish/ international disco. ⓐ Carrer Ramón de Montcada 2 ⓣ 971 69 09 87 ⓑ 24.00–06.00 ⓘ Admission free

⬥ *Crystal-clear waters at Santa Ponça*

Peguera

Peguera is a small but bustling beach resort set around a clear turquoise bay with a pair of golden sandy beaches. The coast road from Peguera to Camp de Mar continues over the mountains to the glitzy marina at Port d'Andratx, another popular hang-out for Mallorca's visiting jet set (see pages 37–39).

BEACHES

Peguera's main beach forms a wide arc of fine sand, with restaurants lining the seafront promenade and plenty of sunbeds and sunshades available for hire. An easy walk of about half an hour leads to the tiny beach at Cala Fornells, beautifully situated inside a crystal-clear cove.

THINGS TO SEE & DO

Glass-bottomed boats
Trips leave regularly from Peguera for Camp de Mar and Port d'Andratx. Some of the trips continue to the village of Sant Elm and the offshore island of Sa Dragonera, now a nature reserve.

TAKING A BREAK

Restaurants & bars
Es Fasset £ A German beer garden with an outdoor, country feel. The restaurant serves pizzas and pasta dishes and the cellar disco plays a mix of English, Spanish and German music. ⓐ Carrer Eucaliptus 5 ⓣ 971 68 71 71 ⓛ 10.00–02.00, live music from 20.00

Obsessions Music Bar £ During the day, snack on tapas, salads and more, and in the evening prepare to be entertained with live music and occasional karaoke nights. There is also a big screen to catch live sports. ⓐ Carrer Eucaliptus 9 ⓣ 628 40 44 21 (mobile) ⓛ 12.00–01.00

La Gran Tortuga ££ Try monkfish stuffed with smoked salmon in spinach sauce. Lovely terrace snack bar. ⓐ Aldea Cala Fornells i Paguera ⓣ 971 68 60 23 ⓛ 13.00–15.30 & 19.30–23.00

Le Plaza ££ Typical Mediterranean cuisine is on offer at this traditional restaurant, including fresh seafood and local meat dishes. Prices are reasonable and service is friendly. ⓐ Carrer Mallorca 4 ⓣ 971 68 77 21 ⓛ 18.30–23.00 Mon, 13.00–16.30 & 18.30–23.00 Tues–Sun

La Gritta £££ Smart restaurant with stunning views. Its menu ranges from classic Spanish dishes such as sea bream baked in a salt crust to Italian specialities like *pansoti*, pasta stuffed with spinach and cheese. ⓐ Carrer L'Espiga 9 ⓣ 971 68 60 22 ⓛ 13.00–23.30; closed Dec & Jan

AFTER DARK

Clubs

Paladium Dance Club 'Life is a Party' promises this nightspot that appeals mostly to the younger crowd, though that can stretch from 18 to 35. Spectacular sound-system laser show. A varied programme of dance music goes along with foam parties and theme nights. Dress is casual. ⓐ Carrer Gaviotas 1 ⓣ 971 68 65 57 ⓦ www.paladiumdisco.es ⓛ 22.00–06.00

SHOPPING

Cambalache This is a long street lined with shops ranging from the trendiest designer fashions to leather accessories, jewellery and arts and crafts.

Le Pirat Jeans are a good buy at this trendy designer-label clothes store. ⓐ Carretera Andratx 3 ⓣ 971 68 53 81

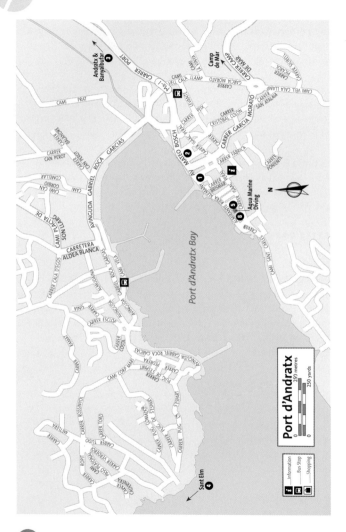

Port d'Andratx

Port d'Andratx (pronounced 'an-dratch') was once a humble fishing village but today it is one of Mallorca's most fashionable resorts, and a great favourite with the yachting fraternity. The picturesque hilly countryside surrounding the port, rich with peach trees, olive groves and vineyards, is also well worth exploring.

Port d'Andratx's character stems from its deep natural harbour – one of the most popular moorings in Mallorca – and its quaysides, lined with all types of craft from traditional fishing boats to massive yachts and ostentatious gin palaces. There is nothing more enjoyable than strolling along the waterfront here, shopping in the chic boutiques, or whiling away the day in one of the sophisticated harbourside restaurants and bars, people-watching and maybe even celebrity-spotting.

The resort also offers visitors a huge range of watersports, but don't come here if you are looking for beaches because you will be disappointed! The best beaches nearby are a short distance along the coast in the neighbouring resorts of **Camp de Mar** and **Sant Elm** (see map opposite). They are easily reached by boat from Port d'Andratx.

Just 4 km (2½ miles) inland, the hilltop town of **Andratx**, surrounded by almond and orange groves, is a must-see. This sleepy town was built away from the coast as a precaution against pirate attack. During the Middle Ages it was the home of both the Catalan King Jaume I and the bishop of Barcelona, hence the massive fortress-like church of Santa María high atop the old town, which commands dazzling views. On Wednesday mornings it comes alive with one of Mallorca's biggest country markets.

The best time to visit Port d'Andratx is just before sunset when the string of popular waterfront cafés and tapas bars which line the promenade come alive and the light is at its best for photographers.

THINGS TO SEE & DO

Boat trips

Hop on a pleasure cruiser and visit the neighbouring resorts of Camp de Mar and Sant Elm, both with their golden sandy beaches. Or try a voyage further afield and take a day trip to Magaluf and Palma Nova. There are also frequent boat trips to the island of Sa Dragonera.

Scuba diving

This part of the coastline offers some of the best scuba diving in Mallorca, with daily courses for both advanced divers and beginners at **Aqua Marine Diving**.

ⓐ Carrer Almirante Riera Alemany 23 ☏ 971 67 43 76 ⏱ Closed mid-Nov–mid-Mar

Walks

Ask in the tourist office for their leaflet on walks around Andratx and explore the countryside. The coastal walks are particularly enjoyable.

EXCURSIONS

The road between Andratx and the small farming community of **Banyalbufar** is one of the best scenic drives in Mallorca, twisting through pretty mountain hamlets high above the craggy northern coastline.

The low-key holiday resort **Camp de Mar**, with Andratx Golf Club (see page 104 for club address) and attractive sandy beach, has become particularly popular with German visitors in recent years. Supermodel Claudia Schiffer is just one of the many Germans to own a luxury home here.

The peaceful holiday resort of **Sant Elm** on the westernmost tip of Mallorca has a sandy beach and attractive harbour as well as several excellent seafood restaurants. The rocky islet of Sa Dragonera is just offshore. Once home to Redbeard the pirate, today it is better known for its variety of seabirds.

TAKING A BREAK

Restaurants & bars
Bar Bellavista £ ❶ The tapas, pizzas and filled rolls at this locals' bar make a pleasant snack lunch beside the old fishing harbour. ⓐ Avinguda Mateo Bosch 31 ❶ 971 67 16 25 ❶ 10.00–22.00

La Consigna £ ❷ This popular cake shop and café serves filled croissants, meat pies and delicious almond cake to eat in or take away, as well as *ensaimadas*, the Mallorcan sugar-sprinkled spiral pastry, straight from the oven. Fresh bread available all day. ⓐ Carrer Mateo Bosch 19 ❶ 971 67 16 25 ❶ 10.00–19.00

Mesón Ca'n Paco ££ ❸ On the road above Andratx, with stunning views of the surrounding hills, is this family-friendly restaurant. In the evenings, local meat and fish are prepared on the outdoor grill. The play area will keep the kids happy. ⓐ Carrer Pedro Seriol 8, Sa Coma ❶ 971 13 79 08 ❶ 12.00–16.00 & 19.00–24.00 Tues–Sun

Na Caragola ££ ❹ A lively restaurant overlooking the island of Sa Dragonera, and serving superb paella and sangría. ⓐ Avinguda Rei Jaume I, Sant Elm ❶ 971 23 90 06 ❶ 12.30–15.30 & 19.00–23.00 Thur–Tues; closed Nov–Jan

Rocamar ££ ❺ Well known for the excellence of its freshly caught fish and shellfish. ⓐ Carrer Almirante Riera Alemany 27 ❶ 971 67 12 61 ❶ 12.30–16.00 & 19.00–23.00 Tues–Sun; closed Nov–Feb

Layn £££ ❻ For a special occasion. A stylish harbourside restaurant with a good choice of meat and fish dishes. Try the gazpacho followed by spaghetti with prawns. Eat on the terrace or on the balcony overlooking the sea. ⓐ Carrer Almirante Riera Alemany 20 ❶ 971 67 18 55 ⓦ www.layn.net ❶ 12.30–15.30 & 19.00–23.00 Tues–Sun; closed Nov–Dec

RESORTS

Cala Sant Vicenç

Cala Sant Vicenç is one of the most perfect spots on the island. Four small coves, each glistening with crystal-clear water, come together beneath the jagged ridge of Cavall Bernat, a magnificent limestone outcrop which casts its shadow into the sea. Although it has become built-up in recent years, it still retains much of its original quiet charm.

BEACHES

Cala Barques and **Cala Molins** each have wide sandy beaches with sunbeds and sunshades for hire. The smaller beach at **Cala Clara** has fewer facilities, while **Cala Carbó** has excellent swimming and snorkelling but no sand. Swimming is safe throughout the resort, but currents can turn strong in stormy weather. Never swim beyond the rope across the entrance to the coves.

THINGS TO SEE & DO

Cala Sant Vicenç Necropolis is a group of man-made caves used for burial purposes some 350 years ago. A hike of around 45 minutes, beginning on the road above **Cala Carbó**, leads across wild countryside to the nearby resort of **Port de Pollença** (see page 43). Another good excursion is to go to **Pollença** (see page 90) for the Sunday-morning market.

TAKING A BREAK

Restaurants & bars
Trotters Bar £ All-day snacks including delicious filled jacket potatoes, pies, haguettes and English bread sandwiches. ⓐ Calle Temporal 31 ● 11.00–23.00 (summer only)

Ca'l Patró ££ Fine sea views to go with its delicious seafood cuisine. Try lobster stew (*caldereta*), or the excellent paella. ⓐ Cala Barques (next to Hotel Niu) ☎ 971 53 38 99 🕐 13.00–15.30 & 20.00–22.30 Wed–Mon; closed Nov–Mar

Pizzeria Cala Sant Vicenç ££ This family-orientated restaurant serves some of the best pizzas in Mallorca, homemade pasta dishes, nachos with mozzarella cheese and take-aways. ⓐ Carrer Temporal 2 ☎ 971 53 02 50 🕐 19.00–23.00

Cavall Bernat £££ Elegant restaurant serving dishes such as quail stuffed with *foie gras*, duck breast with figs and grilled lobster in orange and cinnamon sauce. Expensive but worth it for that special night out. ⓐ Carrer Maressers 2 ☎ 971 53 02 50 🕐 20.00–22.30 Mon–Sat (high season); closed Nov–mid-Mar

AFTER DARK

Bars & clubs
Most resort hotels here provide free entertainment in the evenings. **Trotters Bar** (see opposite) has live music, and the beach bar **Café Art 66** has art exhibitions and DJ sessions. ⓐ Carrer Temporal s/n ☎ 971 53 40 80 🕐 Summer only

⬥ *Beach at Cala Sant Vicenç*

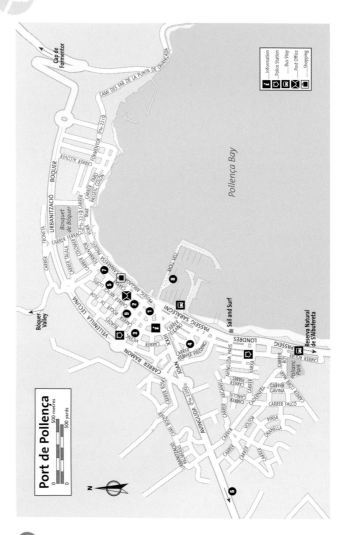

Port de Pollença

Port de Pollença

With a horseshoe-shaped bay and a backdrop of craggy grey mountains, Port de Pollença is one of Mallorca's most attractive resorts. The safe, shallow water and golden sandy beaches make this an especially popular resort for families with young children. Those in search of a more active holiday will find sailing and windsurfing here, as well as some excellent walks to nearby beaches and coves.

Visitors have been coming to Port de Pollença since the 1920s, and the hotels on the seafront have an old-fashioned air. The British crime writer Agatha Christie was one of the earliest visitors and she set one of her short stories in Pollença Bay. Fishing boats are moored beside luxury yachts, and there are numerous tiny beaches which are just the right size for a couple of families each.

BEACHES

The main beach at Port de Pollença stretches into the distance and gets less and less crowded as you move away from the resort towards Alcúdia. A regular bus service connects Port de Pollença with Mallorca's longest beach at Alcúdia (see page 47) and with the other resorts on the northeast coast.

SHOPPING

Aquamarine High-quality handmade jewellery in gold and silver.
ⓐ Carrer Verge del Carme 15
Ceramiques i Decoració Uobrera A wide variety of local ceramics and souvenirs. ⓐ Via Argentina 19 ☎ 971 53 20 81
Papelería Pizell Daily British newspapers, gifts and souvenirs.
ⓐ Carrer Roger de Flor 63 ☎ 971 86 67 90

THINGS TO SEE & DO

Bóquer Valley

A walk of about an hour from Port de Pollença leads past the fortified Bóquer farmhouse across a rugged headland to the shingle beach at Cala Bóquer. On the way you might see wild goats, butterflies and birds, and several varieties of wild flowers. There are no facilities at Cala Bóquer, so take a picnic, plenty of water and sturdy shoes.

Cap de Formentor

Buses and boat trips from Port de Pollença lead to this rocky cape, with stunning views of the wild northeastern coast. Taxi boats run five times a day to Formentor beach, a beautiful white sandy beach.

Reserva Natural de S'Albufereta

These wetlands, located between Pollença and Alcúdia, are very popular with birdwatchers. The area was declared a natural reserve in 2002.

Sailing

Pollença Bay offers ideal conditions for sailing and windsurfing. **Sail and Surf** hires out sailboats and sailboards, and gives lessons to both beginners and the more advanced sailor.

ⓐ Passeig Saralegni ☎ 971 86 53 46

TAKING A BREAK

Restaurants & bars

The Codfather £ ❶ Forgive the terrible pun and enjoy some of the best fish and chips on Mallorca. ⓐ Carrer Ecónom Torres 15 ☎ 971 86 54 24 🕐 09.30–23.30 (Apr–Oct)

Mulligan's Irish Pub £ ❷ Irish and international drinks. Snacks served 12.00–17.00. Live entertainers every Friday, but this place hums every evening. ⓐ Carrer Atilio Boveri 5B ☎ 971 86 75 59 🕐 10.30–04.00

El Posito £ ❸ Really reasonable set menu at lunchtime with a good choice of tapas. ⓐ Carrer Liebieg 8 ❶ 971 86 54 13 ❻ 12.00–15.30 & 19.30–23.30 Mon–Fri, bar 07.00–23.00; closed Dec & Jan

Trotters Bar £ ❹ Great breakfasts and evening meals, steaks, gammon, curries and pies. ⓐ Carrer Temple Fielding 28 ❶ 971 86 46 41 ❻ 11.00–01.00 (summer only)

Na Ruixa ££ ❺ This elegant restaurant is typical of the 'new Mallorcan' style of cooking, providing a fresh twist on traditional recipes. ⓐ Carrer Méndez Núñez 3 ❶ 971 86 66 55 ❻ 13.00–14.00 & 19.00–23.00

Can Cuarassa £££ ❻ Housed in an old Mallorcan mansion just outside Port de Pollença with splendid views. Fresh turbot ravioli with seafood sauce and homemade tiramisú are among the delights on the menu. ⓐ Carretera Port de Pollença-Alcúdia ❶ 971 86 42 66 ❻ 12.00–16.00 & 19.30–22.30

Corb Marí £££ ❼ One of the best restaurants in town, overlooking the sea. Excellent Spanish cuisine and steaks, good value for money. ⓐ Passeig Anglada Camarassa 91 ❶ 971 86 70 40 ⓦ www.restaurantcorbmari.info ❻ 12.30–15.30 & 19.00–22.30 Tues–Sun

La Llonja des Pescador £££ ❽ This restaurant beside the yacht club on the harbour mole serves grilled fish and lobster and an interesting range of meat dishes. ⓐ Moll Vell ❶ 971 86 84 30 ❻ 12.30–16.00 & 19.30–23.00

AFTER DARK

Clubs
Chivas ❾ The main disco in the resort, located near the market square, attracts a good mix of locals and tourists and features equally mixed dance music. ⓐ Carrer Metge Llopis 5 ❻ 23.00–06.00; scratch-and-win cards for free drinks 23.00–01.00 ❗ Admission charge

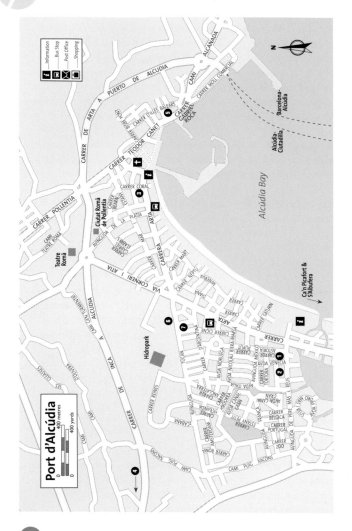

Port d'Alcúdia

The old town of Alcúdia and its port-resort of Port d'Alcúdia merge into each other at the northern tip of sweeping Alcúdia Bay. This is the start of the longest beach on Mallorca, with 10 km (6 miles) of golden sand gently shelving into the water.

The old town itself has been tastefully restored in recent years. Nearly 2,000 years ago this was the capital of Roman Mallorca; the remains of some Roman houses are still visible outside the town walls. The Moors built a new city on the site of the Roman town, and the medieval walls and gates were added after the Spanish conquest in 1229.

The heart of the old town, inside the walls, is now a pleasant pedestrian area of shady streets and ancient mansions, many of them converted into cafés and tapas bars. A lively market is held near here on Tuesday and Sunday mornings.

BEACHES

The stretch from **Port d'Alcúdia** south to **Ca'n Picafort** is one enormous beach, with the kind of sand you dream about, washed by a clear blue sea. There are sunshades and sunbeds for hire, pedaloes to play around in and, if the beach gets too crowded, you can always find a quieter spot further along.

THINGS TO SEE & DO

Hidropark
With its giant water slides, swimming and boating pools, and three mini-golf courses in landscaped surroundings, this aquatic park makes a great day out for all the family. Ask your holiday rep for details of excursions
ⓐ Avinguda de Túcan ❶ 971 89 16 72 ❷ 10.30–18.00 (May–Oct)
❶ Suitable for very young children

Roman Pollentia

There are few visible remains of the Roman city of Pollentia ('power'), perhaps because the islanders have recycled the building materials to create the present town. The **Teatre Romà**, a well-preserved amphitheatre, and **Ciutat Romà de Pollentia**, where Roman houses can be seen, are found off Avinguda de la Platja just outside the medieval walls. The tourist office offers a walk through the Roman town every Wednesday at 10.00 (☎ 971 89 26 15)

S'Albufera

This wetland reserve between Ca'n Picafort and Port d'Alcúdia is an important breeding place for native and migratory birds.
🅐 The entrance is beside the Pont dels Anglesos on the main road to Port d'Alcúdia 🕐 09.00–dusk ❶ Admission free

Excursion

A good excursion by hire car or bicycle is to follow the coast road north of Alcúdia, along the Cap d'es Pinar to the Ermita de la Victoria, a 17th-century hermitage. For an easier bike ride, take the road south of Alcúdia to reach the wetlands at S'Albufera.

TAKING A BREAK

Restaurants & bars
Avinguda de Pere Mas i Reus, in the heart of the resort, is known by the locals as Dollar Street because of its many foreign restaurants and bars.

Cheers £ ❶ This family-orientated bar and restaurant serves a large range of British and international beers, and a wide variety of food. Prices are reasonable and there is a kids' menu. Entertainment is provided for the whole family. 🅐 Avinguda Venecia ☎ 971 89 03 89 🕐 10.00–03.00 There is also a **Cheers 2**. 🅐 Las Gaviotas, Calle Circuito del Lago ☎ 971 89 26 58 🕐 10.00–01.30

Goodfellas £ ② Children are definitely not welcome at this otherwise friendly music and internet café. Live music several times a week and current video releases. **ⓐ** Carrer del Colomí **⏱** Summer only

Sa Taverna £ ③ A medieval townhouse is the setting for this simple but welcoming restaurant. Choose from tapas or tasty charcoal-grilled meat, and finish up with a homemade dessert. **ⓐ** Carrer Serra 9 **☎** 971 54 64 81 **⏱** 11.00–24.00, closed Wed (summer); 12.30–16.00 & 19.00–23.30; closed Wed & Sun (winter)

Bogavante ££ ④ This top-notch seafood restaurant is situated opposite the fishermen's pier with delightful views of the harbour. Stuffed mussels and mixed seafood grill are two of the house specialities. **ⓐ** Carrer Teodor Canet 2 **☎** 971 54 73 64 **⏱** 13.00–16.00 & 19.00–23.00 Tues–Sun; closed mid-Nov–Dec

AFTER DARK

Bars & clubs

Magic ⑤ There is a different theme every night at this hugely popular club. DJs spin everything from r'n'b to house. There are foam parties, circus nights and much, much more. **ⓐ** Avinguda de Túcan **⏱** From 22.00 (summer)

Menta ⑥ Alcúdia's biggest and most popular nightclub, modelled on a Roman temple, features an indoor heated swimming pool, plus two DJs and seven bars. The music is a mixture of Spanish and disco music. **ⓐ** Avinguda de Tucán 6 **☎** 971 89 19 72 **ⓦ** www.mentadisco.com **⏱** 22.00–06.00 **❶** Admission charge

Mestizo Café £ ⑦ Regular gigs on Tuesday nights make this bar a hit with both tourists and locals. They serve sandwiches and light snacks as well as cocktails and other refreshments. **ⓐ** Carrer Coral s/n **☎** 971 89 72 70 **⏱** 20.00–03.00 Mon, 16.00–03.00 Tues–Sun

Cala Ratjada

Cala Ratjada manages to be two things at once; a genuine fishing port, and a busy resort where watersports are the main attraction. This delightful stretch of coastline is studded with small coves, each with their own sandy beach.

BEACHES

Font de Sa Cala, 5 km (3 miles) south of the resort, has clean water and gently shelving sand and is ideal for both swimming and sunbathing. Every kind of watersport is available here. **Son Moll** is popular with young families, while north of the resort are the attractive, quieter beaches of **Cala Guya**, **Cala Agulla** and **Cala Mesquida**.

THINGS TO SEE & DO

Artà
Take the bus from Cala Ratjada to the delightful inland town of **Artà**, crowned by the hilltop sanctuary of **Sant Salvador**.

Coves d'Artà (Artà Caves)
These magnificent underground rock formations lie a few kilometres south of Cala Ratjada, close to the small resort of Canyamel. The one-hour guided tour comes complete with dazzling special effects.
❶ 971 84 12 93 ⓦ www.cuevasdearta.com ⏲ 10.00–18.00 (May–Oct); 10.00–17.00 (Nov–Apr) ❶ Admission charge

Jardins Casa March (Casa March Gardens)
The Mallorcan banker Joan March was a great collector of modern art and the gardens of his country home have been turned into a sculpture park. Evening concerts take place here every July. Visits by arrangement with the Tourist Office.
ⓐ Plaça dels Pins ❶ 971 56 30 33

Punta de Capdepera

A scenic 3-km (2-mile) walk from the centre of the resort leads to the lighthouse at Punta de Capdepera, the easternmost point on Mallorca.

TAKING A BREAK

Restaurants

Ca'n Cardaix ££ Totally unpretentious and original. Bare floors, wooden benches, no tablecloths, no traffic, so the kids can run around while you eat good, well-cooked food in peace. ⓐ Avinguda Canyamel, Font de Sa Cala ⓣ 971 56 30 88 ⓛ 11.00–16.00 & 19.00 until late

Ses Rotges £££ The top restaurant in the resort serves quality French cuisine in the backstreets behind the port. ⓐ Carrer Rafael Blanes 21 ⓣ 971 56 31 08 ⓛ 19.30–22.30

AFTER DARK

Clubs

Physical Smart but casual defines the dress code at this popular disco. There is a laser show as well as regular foam parties. ⓐ Carrer des Coconar 17 ⓛ 23.00–06.00 ❶ Admission charge

● *The harbour at Cala Ratjada*

Cala Bona & Cala Millor

Most of Mallorca's east coast is dotted with tiny creeks and coves, but at Cala Millor the golden sands just go on and on, stretching for more than 1 km (½ mile) along a wide, sheltered bay.

Cala Millor, with restaurants and bars lining its seafront promenade, is one long party in summer. Cala Bona, still based around its old fishing harbour, is a quieter resort with a smaller beach and a rather more laid-back atmosphere.

The best way to appreciate the feel of these two resorts is to walk from Cala Millor to Cala Bona in the early evening, along the seafront Passeig Marítim which connects the two, ending up at the harbour for a drink in one of the many waterside bars. Follow this with a seafood dinner at the port, and by the time you have walked back you will be ready to sample Cala Millor's nightlife.

BEACHES

The beach at **Cala Millor** has clear water, gently sloping sand, sunshades and sunbeds for hire and watersports facilities and is safe for young children. You can touch the bottom up to 100 m (330 ft) out. **Cala Bona**'s cove-like beach is smaller, but with similar facilities. Seaweed can be a problem here.

THINGS TO SEE & DO

Boat tours
Glass-bottomed boats from Cala Millor tour the scenic east coast, north to Cala Ratjada (see page 50) and south to Portocristo (see page 58).

Fantasy Park
This outdoor play area near the centre of Cala Millor is paradise for children, with rides and inflatables for toddlers and older children alike.
ⓐ By the Parc de la Mar gardens ⓒ 10.00–21.00 ❶ Admission charge

⬤ *The dream-like Cala Millor*

Pirate Ship

Stops at Sa Coma, S'Illot, Portocristo and Cala Vaquace, which can only be reached by sea. Lunch on board.
ⓐ Boat tours depart from Passeig Marítim, Cala Millor ❶ 639 65 48 48 (mobile)

Safari-Zoo

See giraffes, zebra, elephants and monkeys at this miniature safari park between Cala Millor and Sa Coma. You can drive around the 4-km (2½-mile) circuit in your own car or take the zoo's mini-train. Get there from Cala Bona or Cala Millor on the Safari Bus or the little road train.
❶ 971 81 09 09 🕐 09.00–19.00 (Apr–Sept), 09.00–17.00 (Oct–Mar)
❶ Admission charge

Torre de n'Amer (n'Amer Tower)

You can walk up to this medieval watchtower on the headland of Punta de n'Amer, with spectacular views out to sea and back down over the

resort. The walk takes around 45 minutes and there is a bar at the top selling drinks and snacks.
ⓐ Between Cala Millor and Sa Coma

TAKING A BREAK

Restaurants & bars

Bar Nàutic £ This café-bar overlooking Cala Bona's port attracts locals as well as visitors and serves snacks such as hamburgers, rolls and *pa amb oli* (see page 95). ⓐ Avinguda de n'Antoni Garau Mulet 21, Cala Bona ⓣ 971 58 60 27 ⓛ 10.00 until late, closed Mon (winter)

Cheer's Bar £ Warm, friendly and British-owned, Cheer's serves great homemade food including roast dinners, as well as sandwiches and snacks. There are big-screen TVs for the sports, a cinema terrace for kids, karaoke, darts and lots more. ⓐ Carrer Son Corb 20, Cala Millor ⓣ 971 58 60 79 ⓛ 09.30–03.00

Sanddancers £ A lively bar that is a great place for families, with activities and entertainment every night. The list extends to sporting events, bingo, quizzes and karaoke, and there is an extensive play area and a cinema for the kids. ⓐ Carrer de Na Llambies 81, Cala Bona ⓣ 971 58 72 43 ⓛ 11.00 until late

Bon Gust ££ Specialises in Mediterranean Mallorquín cuisine, fresh fish and paella. They also serve a *fideuà paella* (with pasta instead of rice) and a variety of pasta dishes. The menu includes tapas and many other interesting dishes, all at reasonable prices. ⓐ Carrer Es Rafal 3, Cala Millor ⓣ 971 58 59 30 ⓛ 12.00–16.00 & 19.00–24.00 Tues–Sun

Fonoll Marí ££ This friendly seafood restaurant overlooks the waterfront in Cala Bona. It is a good place to try the typical local dish *frit Mallorquí* (chopped potatoes fried up with meat and herbs) as well as fresh fish and paellas. ⓐ Passeig de Moll 24, Cala Bona ⓣ 971 81 36 41 ⓛ 13.00–15.30 & 18.30–23.30, closed Mon (low season), closed mid-Nov to early Mar

Nou Candil ££ This simple and unpretentious restaurant prides itself on its good, old-fashioned Mallorcan cooking. Everything is locally sourced and beautifully fresh, from the fresh fish of the day to the tasty veggie dishes (which include a vegetarian paella). ⓐ Avinguda Cristobal Colon 92, Cala Millor ⓣ 971 58 74 27 ⓛ 13.00–16.00 & 19.00–24.00 Thur–Tues

Son Floriana £££ This Mallorcan country house in the quiet back roads of Cala Bona is known for its reliable cuisine. Specialities include mixed paella and Chateaubriand steak, and the wine cellar has a fine selection of Mallorcan and Spanish wines. ⓐ Avinguda de Las Magnòlia, Cala Bona ⓣ 971 58 60 75 ⓛ 13.00–15.00 & 19.00–24.00

AFTER DARK

Bars
With its low-key nightlife, Cala Bona is not for the clubbers of this world, but there are plenty of bars to choose from in the harbour area, some with live music. A 20-minute walk will take you to vibrant Cala Millor, lined with bars and clubs.

La Havana
Start the night with a caipirinha on the terrace at La Havana, one of the best-known disco bars in Cala Millor, then stick around as DJs spin upbeat summer tunes from Spanish pop to the latest dance music. ⓐ Carrer Llum s/n ⓦ www.la-havana.es. ⓛ 20.30–late Apr–Sept. Check opening dates and times (which vary annually) on the website

Sa Coma & S'Illot

These two resorts, each with their own sandy beach, are separated by a small rocky headland. They have everything you need for a relaxing family holiday.

THINGS TO SEE & DO

Golf
Children will happily spend all day at **Golf Paradis**, a 54-hole mini-golf course, set in a make-believe landscape.
🅐 Carrer las Lilas s/n, off Avinguda de les Palmeres 🕿 971 81 10 02
🕙 10.00–23.00; closed Nov–Apr

Safari-Zoo
See giraffes, zebra, elephants and monkeys at this miniature safari park, on the road between Sa Coma and Cala Millor. You can get there from Sa Coma and S'Illot on the free Safari Bus (see page 53 for more details).
🕿 971 81 09 09 🕙 09.00–19.00, until 17.00 in winter ❶ Admission charge

Torre de n'Amer (n'Amer Tower)
It takes around 45 minutes to walk up to this medieval watchtower and enjoy its spectacular views. There is a bar at the top selling drinks and snacks (see pages 53–4 for more details).

TAKING A BREAK

Restaurants & bars
BiBaBo £ Families are welcome at this very good-value café and music

> ### SHOPPING
> The **Caprabo** hypermarket on Avinguda de les Palmeres is a good place to stock up on food, including fresh seafood.

bar. The food is a mixture of Spanish and British. ⓐ Passeig Neptú 11, S'Illot ⓣ 971 81 01 60 ⓛ 08.30–23.00; closed Oct–Apr

Es Cuerot ££ A cellar restaurant serving traditional Mallorcan cuisine, such as the *frit mallorquí*, a fry-up of meat and vegetables. ⓐ Carrer Dàlies, Sa Coma ⓣ 971 81 02 80 ⓛ 09.00–16.00 & 18.00–24.00

Lago £££ A top-notch restaurant serving Spanish and Mallorcan cuisine. The mixed seafood platter and fillet steak in Roquefort sauce are both highly recommended. ⓐ Carrer Mitjorn 9, S'Illot ⓣ 971 81 02 09 ⓛ 12.30–15.30 & 19.00–23.30; closed Dec–Jan

AFTER DARK

Bars & clubs
Crazy Monkeys Music bar with a monkey theme and a laid-back atmosphere. Spanish-style cocktail bar. ⓐ Rosa dels Vents, S'Illot ⓛ Happy Hour 20.00–23.00 & 24.00–02.00

Espace Don't get left behind in the rush for the only disco in Sa Coma and S'Illot. The dress code is casual. ⓐ Carrer Rosa dels Vents, S'Illot ⓣ 971 81 09 93 ⓛ 22.00–06.00

ⓐ *Windsurfers on the beach*

Portocristo

With a wide sandy beach at the end of a long curving bay, Portocristo is a favourite. Sailors are drawn here by its calm, sheltered waters, and the marina is a good place for spotting luxury yachts. It has one of Mallorca's leading family attractions, the Coves del Drac. There is not an extensive range of shops or restaurants but this is a characterful resort ideal for holiday-makers and small children.

THINGS TO SEE & DO

Coves del Drac (Dragon Caves)

A trip to these caves is one of the highlights of any holiday on Mallorca. You walk along 2 km (1¼ miles) of paths inside vast underground caverns, gazing at stalactites that have formed into eerie shapes over the centuries. The caves are illuminated and the icing on the cake is a concert of classical music as you ride on a boat across Lake Martel, Europe's largest underground lake.

ⓐ Just outside Portocristo on the road to Cales de Mallorca

ⓣ 971 82 07 53 ⓛ 10.00–17.00 (Apr–Oct); 10.45–12.00 & 14.00–15.30 (Nov–Mar); (tours 10.45, 12.00, 15.30, without music 16.30)

ⓘ Admission charge

Coves dels Hams (Caves of Hams)

Just outside Portocristo, they are not as big as the Coves del Drac but still enjoyable.

ⓐ On the road to Manacor ⓣ 971 82 09 88 ⓛ 10.00–18.00 (Mar–Oct); 10.30–17.30 (Nov–Feb) ⓘ Admission charge

Mallorca Aquàrium

A small aquarium with exotic fish from around the world, including piranhas, poisonous puffer fish and electric eels.

ⓐ Carrer de la Vela, near the Coves del Drac ⓣ 971 82 09 71

ⓛ 10.30–18.30 (Apr–Oct); 11.00–15.00 (Nov–Mar) ⓘ Admission charge

● *Beach at Portocristo*

TAKING A BREAK

Restaurants
Golden Bay £ This is a delightful spot to relax, watching the small boats plying back and forth. Cantonese and Shanghai cooking. ❸ Carrer Paseo Rivet 25, Portocristo ❶ 971 82 25 05 ❺ 11.00–16.00 & 18.00–24.00

Cap d'es Toi ££ This popular restaurant specialises in fresh fish and meat dishes. There is a choice of homemade pizzas and 50 varieties of *pa amb oli* (see page 95). ❸ Passeig es Riuet s/n, Portocristo ❶ 971 82 25 78 ❺ 12.00–23.00 (Feb–Oct)

Club Náutico ££ This seafood restaurant has a prime position overlooking the marina, making it the best place in the resort for a special treat. The house speciality is paella. ❸ Carrer de la Vela 29 ❶ 971 82 02 99 ❺ 12.00–14.30 & 19.30–23.00

Sa Llonja £££ A smart, modern restaurant overlooking the port. The speciality is seafood, brought in daily from their own fishing boats. Finish up with Mallorcan almond cake (*gato*). ❸ Passeig Moll 1, Portocristo ❶ 971 82 28 59 ❺ 09.00–20.00 (June–Sept); 12.30–17.00 & 19.30–24.00 (Oct–Nov & Feb–May); closed Dec and Jan

Cales de Mallorca

Cales de Mallorca is the collective name for around 20 small coves that dot the coastline between Portocristo and Porto Colom. Many of them can only be reached by boat, but three of the larger coves form the setting for a small, self-contained resort – also known as Cales de Mallorca. Many of the hotels here operate on an 'all-inclusive' basis and there are comparatively few shops, bars and restaurants. Although it may not suit those looking for nightlife, this resort is very child-oriented, with lots for children to do.

Each of the three bays – Cala Antena, Cala Domingos Grans and Cala Domingos Petits – has its own sandy beach. The Calas Express road train trundles between the beaches, but if you are feeling energetic you should take the coastal path for its stunning clifftop views, especially at dawn. Most of the action 'downtown', including shops and restaurants, is found in the Centro Comercial, a shopping centre with a mini-golf course and sandy play area at its centre.

THINGS TO SEE & DO

Boat trips

A glass-bottomed boat trip along the fjord-like east coast, with its secluded beaches and pine-fringed coves, is a must. Some of the trips stop at Portocristo, giving you time to visit the Coves del Drac (Dragon Caves, see page 58). Others visit the pretty sand and shingle beach at Cala Murada, just south of Cales de Mallorca.

Jumaica gardens

In this tropical garden and banana plantation, you will find birds flying free, pools, cascades and a restaurant/bar.
ⓐ Carretera Porto Colom–Portocristo, Km 4.5 ❶ 971 83 33 55
🕐 09.00–18.00 (summer); 10.00–16.00 (winter); restaurant closed Mon
❶ Admission charge

TAKING A BREAK

Restaurants & bars

La Macarena £ A friendly Spanish bar overlooking the children's play-ground, with a good selection of traditional tapas. ⓐ Centro Comercial ⓣ 971 83 32 34 ⓛ 10.00–01.00

Mar Azul £ This café, with live music three times a week, serves simple, good-value meals. ⓐ Carrer de Lala Antena ⓣ 971 83 32 10 ⓛ 09.00–15.30 & 18.00–22.30

Marítimo £ This restaurant overlooking the beach has a water-slide, a children's playground and pool, and serves everything from paella to grilled sole and chips. ⓐ Platja Domingos Grans ⓣ 971 83 37 96 ⓛ 10.00–18.00

Bar Mallorca ££ This Spanish bar serves paella, pizzas and pasta dishes on a covered patio. The crazy-golf course outside is operated by the bar,

● *Boats at Cales de Mallorca*

so you can watch your children play while you tuck in. ⓐ Centro Comercial ⓣ 971 83 32 17 ⓛ 09.00–23.30

Ca'n Pep Noguera ££ Classic Mallorcan cooking in a romantic setting, just outside the resort. House specialities include *arròs brut*, a Mallorcan version of paella. ⓐ Carretera Portocristo–Porto Colom ⓣ 971 83 33 55 ⓛ 12.30–16.00 & 19.00–23.00 Tues–Sun

Casa Pila ££ This is a typically British joint serving English breakfast, roast dinner and homemade pies. ⓐ Carrer Formentor s/n (Centro Comercial) ⓣ 649 15 55 31 (mobile) ⓛ 09.00–15.00 & 18.30–22.30 Tues–Sun

Maysi ££ Roast lamb and grilled prawns are two of the specialities at this good-value restaurant. You dine on a covered patio with sea views. ⓐ Centro Comercial ⓣ 971 88 33 43 ⓛ 11.30–23.00

Oriente City ££ This Chinese restaurant serves classic Cantonese cooking, such as sweet and sour chicken and beef in oyster sauce, on a shady terrace in a quiet backstreet. ⓐ Cala Romaguera ⓣ 971 83 41 67 ⓛ 12.30–16.00 & 18.30–24.00

Pizzeria d'Alfil ££ A very popular family-oriented restaurant serving pizzas, pasta and cocktails on an outdoor terrace with a fountain. There is live music plus a DJ or entertainer here most nights. ⓐ Passeig de Manacor s/n (Centro Comercial) ⓣ 971 83 40 88 ⓛ 11.00–04.00

SHOPPING

The shops are concentrated at the Centro Comercial. Try **Carolyn** for jewellery, including Majorica pearls, **Euro-Perfumería Eden** for duty-free perfumes and **Casa Pila Sports** for sports gear and swimwear. For local arts and crafts, head into nearby **Felanitx** for its Sunday morning market.

CALES DE MALLORCA

Sol y Vida ££ This upmarket air-conditioned restaurant is the ideal place to sample traditional Basque and Spanish food. Its Pub, **La Cueva**, is a small, intimate bar with an outside terrace, located on the clifftop with sweeping sea views, where you can eat or sit and have a drink at any time of day. ⓐ Manzana F37 Cala Murada ① 971 83 31 70 ② 11.00–24.00

AFTER DARK

Bars & clubs
The resort's main square is the place to be at night, with pavement artists, buskers and hair-braiders in the street and plenty of entertainment in the bars around it.

Flamingos This bar caters to all tastes in music and has a satellite TV and a pool table. ⓐ Carrer Cala Romaguera ② 19.00 until late; Happy Hour 22.00–01.00

Jupiter It's mostly British dance music at this lively bar-disco, which only really gets into full swing after midnight. Children welcome. ⓐ Cala Romaguera ② 20.00–03.00

Rock Cola This is the largest bar in town. Special barbecues, ice creams and Rock Cola cocktails. Party atmosphere. Live entertainment every evening followed by disco, with the only top international professional DJ in the resort. ⓐ Cales de Mallorca ① 650 43 38 78 ② 16.00–04.00 (May–Oct); Happy Hour 20.00–01.00

Le Saint Louis Serves great cocktails and has a lively atmosphere at night. ⓐ Centro Comercial ② 18.00 until late

Tiffany's There's a varied mix of music styles to suit the international clientele of this nightclub. The age group ranges from 20 to 40 and there is no specific dress code. ⓐ Cala Romaguera ② 24.00–06.00 ❶ Under-18s are not allowed

Porto Colom

The fishing village of Porto Colom was named in honour of Christopher Columbus who, it is said, was born here. Set around a natural harbour, the resort still has the feel of a small fishing port and is ideal for a peaceful, relaxing holiday for families with young children.

Porto Colom was once the port for the nearby town of Felanitx, and thrived by exporting Mallorcan wine to France. However, when phylloxera (a kind of insect) killed the island's vineyards, its role as a port diminished.

Porto Colom is the ideal setting for all watersports, and the best beach is located 2 km (1¼ miles) to the south, in the quiet resort of **Cala Marçal**. Keen walkers will enjoy exploring the Serra de Llevant mountain range, with its spectacular views. Its highest points are crowned by the 14th-century **Ermita de Sant Salvador** (Hermitage of St Salvador) and the ancient **Castell de Santueri** (Castle of Sanctuary).

THINGS TO SEE & DO

Boat trips
Exploring the Porto Colom coastline aboard a glass-bottomed boat is always a fun day out for all the family.

Golf
In the hills just a short distance from the resort, this challenging 18-hole **Vall d'Or** golf course has spectacular views from the fairways and welcome sea breezes in summer.
ⓐ Carretera Porto Colom–Cala d'Or, Km 7.7 ⓣ 971 83 70 01
ⓦ www.valldorgolf.com ⓛ All year

Horse riding
Spend a splendid day trekking in the countryside with Escola d'Equitació Son Menut. You can even ride to the Consolacíon Sanctuary or visit a castle for lunch.
ⓐ Camí de Son Negre, Felanitx ⓣ 971 58 29 20 ⓦ www.sonmenut.com

TAKING A BREAK

Restaurants & bars

Bar Citrus £ Wide range of local and imported beers. Barbecue every night in summer. ⓐ Carrer Assumpció 20 ⓣ 971 82 40 59 ⓛ 11.00–late.

Bob's Restaurant £ Homemade food such as lasagne, all-day English breakfasts, pies and grills. Live music most nights. ⓐ Plaça C'as Corso 15 ⓛ 09.00–15.00 & 18.00–01.00; closed Nov–Easter

Club Naùtic de Porto Colom ££ The sea views are the perfect complement to the fresh seafood and the Mallorcan dishes. ⓐ Carrer Pescadors 31 ⓣ 971 82 62 34 ⓛ 13.00–15.30 & 19.30–22.00 Tues–Sun

Restaurant Plaza ££ A cheerful café with a terrace on a palm-tree-shaded square, this is a great option for families. ⓐ Plaça Ca's Corso ⓣ 971 82 40 21 ⓛ 11.00–01.00; closed Jan–Mar

Florian £££ Stylish and fashionable restaurant serving contemporary Mediterranean cuisine. Three-course lunch menu for under €15. ⓐ Carrer Cristobal Colom 11 ⓣ 971 82 41 71 ⓛ 11.00–17.00 & 19.00–until late; closed Thur (low season), closed Nov–Mar

Sa Sinia £££ Sa Sinia serves fine Mallorcan cuisine. ⓐ Carrer Pescadors s/n ⓣ 971 82 43 23 ⓛ 13.30–15.30 and 19.00–22.30 Tues–Sun

AFTER DARK

Bars & clubs

Calipso Porto Colom's only disco attracts a young crowd, eager to party. ⓐ Carrer d'Hernán Cortés ⓛ 23.00–06.00

Pay-pay There's often live music outside this popular Polynesian-style cocktail bar. ⓐ Plaça Corsa ⓛ 17.00–03.00

Cala d'Or

This chic resort has grown over the years to embrace several of the nearby creeks and coves.

Cala d'Or is one of the liveliest resorts on the east coast, with most of the action taking place in and around the marina. To the north and south stretches a succession of rocky coves, where small resorts have gradually grown up around fine sandy beaches: Cala Serena, Cala Egos, Cala Barca and Portopetro. Cala Mondragó, south of Cala d'Or, has twin beaches connected by a clifftop path. You can travel between all of these coves on the Cala d'Or Express, a mini-train running between Cala Serena and Cala Mondragó in summer.

BEACHES

Cala Gran, close to the centre of the resort, is the largest beach. Near here is **Cala d'Or** itself, a pine-fringed cove with a small but crowded white-sand beach. Sunbeds, sunshades and pedaloes can be hired at both of these beaches, and also at **Cala Mondragó**, **Cala Egos** and **Cala Barca**.

THINGS TO SEE & DO

Excursions
Cala Figuera
This charming village, a few kilometres south of Cala d'Or, is still very much a fishing port, with fishermen's cottages lining the narrow inlet. There are several arts and crafts shops in the village as well as some excellent seafood restaurants.

Es Trenc
Spreading northwest from Colònia de Sant Jordi, this is a protected area where no development is allowed. The beautiful beach stretches for almost 5 km (3 miles). There is a small bar-restaurant here. Be aware, though, that Es Trenc is popular with nudists.

Portopetro

This fishing village has retained its old-world character, with its traditional fishing boats, picturesque port and charming whitewashed fishermen's cottages.

Sa Colònia de Sant Jordi

Once the haunt of pirates and smugglers, this is one of Mallorca's quieter seaside resorts, with a pocket-handkerchief-sized beach. There are also daily boat trips at 09.30 from Sa Colònia's port to the island of Cabrera – a protected National Land-Sea Park.

TAKING A BREAK

Restaurants & bars

Brasserie Rouge £ Brit favourites including jacket potatoes and steak platters. There is a great cheap menu for kids and several screens for sports. ⓐ Avinguda Boulevard d'Or 63, Cala d'Or ⓣ 679 28 10 16 (mobile) ⓛ 09.00 until late

The Duke of Devonshire £ A classic British pub with a play area for kids and an outdoor terrace. They offer home-cooked meals and snacks,

⬤ *The chic resort of Cala d'Or*

including plenty of options for veggies. 🅐 Carrer Espalmador 165, Cala d'Or 🕿 971 65 98 44 🕒 09.30–02.30; closed Nov–Apr

San Lorenzo £ Italian cooking with the emphasis on fresh produce. Family friendly. 🅐 Carrer Cristofor Colom 99, Portopetro 🕿 971 65 81 71 🕒 12.00–16.00 (for buffet) & 18.30 until late; closed Tues

Blanco y Negro ££ Popular seafood restaurant by the marina. 🅐 Marina de Cala d'Or 🕿 971 64 34 65 🕒 12.00–23.30; closed end Oct–Easter

Cala ££ Excellent fish restaurant. 🅐 Carrer Virgen del Carmen, Cala Figuera 🕿 971 64 50 18 🕒 09.00–22.30

Ca'n Trompé ££ Hugely popular Mallorcan restaurant that serves an excellent-value three-course menu. 🅐 Avinguda de Bélgica 12, Cala d'Or 🕿 971 65 73 41 🕒 12.30–15.30 & 19.00–23.30; closed end Nov–early Feb

Don Leone ££ Pizzas and pasta dishes are freshly made to order. 🅐 Carrer Toni Costa 13, Cala d'Or 🕿 971 64 34 14 🕒 12.00–24.00; closed end Oct–Easter

El Lazo ££ The mixed grill is highly recommended at this meat-oriented Spanish restaurant. There's a big menu for kids and the prices are reasonable. 🅐 Carrer Toni Costa 23, Cala d'Or 🕿 971 65 74 38 🕒 12.00–15.00 & 18.00–23.00

Portopetro ££ One of the port's top fish restaurants, with fantastic views over the fishing harbour. 🅐 Passeig d'es Port 49, Portopetro 🕿 971 65 77 04 🕒 11.30–16.00 & 18.30–23.30; closed lunch Tues, closed Nov–early Mar

Bona Taula £££ Intimate and elegant for a special occasion. Mallorcan dishes. 🅐 Rafael Adrover 32, Cala d'Or 🕿 971 16 71 47 🕒 19.00–23.00 Wed–Mon

Port Petit £££ This upmarket restaurant overlooking the marina specialises in seafood, including Mediterranean rock lobster. ⓐ Marina de Cala d'Or ⓣ 971 64 30 39 ⓛ 13.00–15.30 & 19.00–23.00; closed Tues lunch (summer) and Tues all day (winter)

AFTER DARK

Bars & clubs
Chic Palace Charts and house music for 20-somethings. ⓐ Plaça Costa 1, Cala d'Or ⓣ 971 65 97 94 ⓛ 23.00–07.00 ⓘ Admission charge

Club Passion Electric atmosphere. 'Anything goes' attitude positively encouraged. ⓐ Carrer S'Espalmador 3, Cala d'Or ⓛ 22.00 until late

Hollywood Bar A very popular karaoke bar with quizzes, DJs and other entertainment every night. ⓐ Carrer Ravells 11, Cala d'Or ⓣ 971 65 98 52 ⓛ 17.00 until late, closed Nov–Apr

Mondbar Superb cocktails and a fantastic open-air dance floor. ⓐ Carrer Pintor Bernareggi, Cala Figuera ⓛ 20.30 until late

Pinte A popular pint-sized jazz bar. ⓐ Carrer Pintor Bernareggi, Cala Figuera ⓛ 19.30–03.00

Shhh...Bar An elegant bar which serves good cocktails and drinks. There's a PlayStation for the kids. ⓐ Carrer Port Petite, Marina ⓣ 971 64 80 77 ⓛ 17.00 until late (Apr–Oct), Thurs–Sun 17.00 until late (rest of the year)

SHOPPING
The Sunday morning market in the nearby town of **Felanitx** is one of the best in Mallorca. This is a good place to pick up some local pottery. Visit **Cala Figuera** for pottery, glass and Lladró sculptures.

S'Arenal

The bustling resort of S'Arenal sits at one end of the long Platja de Palma, a stretch of more than 5 km (3 miles) of wide sandy beach, with the twin resort of Ca'n Pastilla at the other end. The resorts have a highly international flavour, with English pubs, German and Dutch bars.

There is plenty in S'Arenal to keep everyone amused, with facilities for windsurfing and water-skiing as well as pedalo hire. Children can splash safely around in the shallow water, and there are also a number of playgrounds. A palm-lined promenade runs the length of the resort, offering good views across Palma Bay.

THINGS TO SEE & DO

Aqualand
One of the largest water parks on the Med, Aqualand has enough thrills and spills to keep children busy all day. One of the rides is called The Devil's Tail (La Cola del Diablo) and another Kamikaze, though there are more sedate rides. It's a great day out for all the family, with go-karting, parrot shows and a mini-farm.
ⓐ Beside Palma–S'Arenal motorway, exit 13 (15 minutes' walk from S'Arenal)
ⓣ 971 44 00 00 ⓛ 10.00–18.00 (July & Aug); 10.00–17.00 (May, June & Sept); closed Oct–Apr ❶ Admission charge (free for under-3s)

Golf Fantasia
Play fantasy golf at three 18-hole putting courses in a landscape of caves, waterfalls and tropical gardens with dinosaurs.
ⓐ Carretera del Arenal 56 (between Balneario 4 & 5) ⓣ 971 74 33 34
ⓛ 09.30–02.30

Palma Aquárium
Opened in 2007, this aquarium complex is one of the biggest in Europe, with over 700 different species in 55 aquariums. The highlight is a tunnel through the enormous shark tanks.

📍 Carrer Manuel de los Herreros i Sora 2 ☎ 971 74 61 88
🌐 www.palmaaquarium.com 🕐 10.00–18.00 ❗ Admission charge

TAKING A BREAK

Restaurants & bars
The Sportsman £ This classic pub on the seafront offers great British grub, including full English breakfasts and roast dinners. It is crammed with all kinds of sporting memorabilia, and big screens ensure you'll never miss a single sporting event. 📍 Carrer Miramar ☎ 971 44 30 61 🕐 10.00 until late, closed Nov–Apr

Can Torrat ££ An open-air ranch-style restaurant popular with Mallorcans who head here at weekends for platefuls of barbecued meat. 📍 Camí de las Meravelles ☎ 971 26 20 55 🕐 13.00–03.00, closed Wed

Ca's Cotxer ££ Generous portions of Mallorcan classics, with an emphasis on fresh fish and seafood. 📍 Carretera del Arenal 31 ☎ 971 26 20 49 🕐 13.00–16.00 & 19.00–24.00

Molí de Can Pere £££ Converted 1631 mill with rustic tables in a delightful courtyard. Specialities include rabbit, suckling pig and lamb. 📍 Carrer S'Arenal-Llucmajor, Km 1 🕐 13.00–16.00 & 19.30–02.00; closed Mon

AFTER DARK

Clubs
RIU-Palace One of Mallorca's top nightspots, with room for 2,000 people in a giant disco. House/dance music, go-go dancers, laser show. 📍 Carrer del Llaut 🕐 22.00–06.00

Zorba's An international disco with a youngish clientele. Dance/house music, two stages, 11 bars and room for 4,000 people! The locals flock here at weekends too. 📍 Avinguda de Son Rigo 🕐 22.00–06.00

Ca'n Pastilla & Platja de Palma

Ideal for families young and old, days are spent lazing on the 7-km (4½-mile) beach or taking part in the many watersports on offer. At night, choose between a drink at one of the many bars or enjoying a meal on the seafront overlooking the beautiful bay of Palma.

TAKING A BREAK

Restaurants & bars
Ricky's Tavern £ Good British grub including full breakfasts and homemade specialities, plus nightly quizzes and a karaoke night.
ⓐ Avinguda Bartolome Riutort ⏰ 10.30–15.00 & 20.00–01.00

El Rancho Picadero ££ Not for vegetarians. Meat is grilled over a wood fire and served on a beautiful garden terrace. ⓐ Carrer del Flamenco, Ca'n Pastilla ☎ 971 26 10 02 ⏰ 13.00–24.00

Anima Sea Lounge £££ Stylish restaurant with an eclectic menu from Mediterranean classics to Japanese sushi. ⓐ Carrer Pins 17, Cala Estancia ☎ 971 74 54 37 ⏰ 13.00–16.00 (mid-July–Oct); closed Mon (Nov–mid-July)

AFTER DARK

Bars & clubs
Buskers Not to be missed. Jam sessions with professional entertainers. Buskers during the day. ⓐ Carrer Bellamar ⏰ All day until late

Puro Beach Mingle with the jet set at this ultra-fashionable beachfront chill-out bar. White sunbeds circle a perfect pool and everyone comes dressed to impress. Pricey but worth it. ⓐ Cala Estancia ☎ 971 74 47 44 ⓦ www.purohotel.com ⏰ 11.00 until late (summer); closed winter

▶ *The Monastery of Valldemossa where Chopin spent a winter*

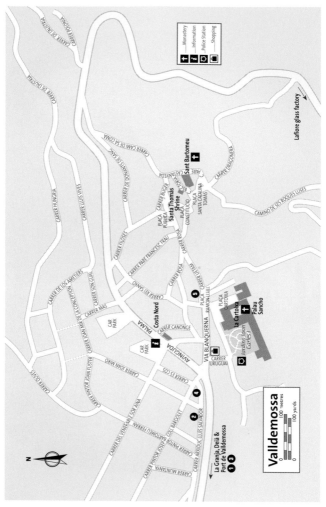

Valldemossa

Valldemossa (pronounced 'Val-de-moss-er') is one of the best-known mountain villages in Mallorca. Here Frédéric Chopin and his mistress George Sand (real name Aurore Dudevant, born Dupin) spent the winter of 1838–9 in the Cartoixa (Charterhouse). The monastery and scenery have changed little since, and Valldemossa remains well worth visiting, if only for the monastic peace after the bustle of Mallorca's beach resorts.

Chopin and the French novelist Sand came to Mallorca to escape the gossip of Paris, and in the hope that the mild climate would improve Chopin's health. However, Chopin's piano failed to arrive, his health deteriorated and so did their relationship. Afterwards, Sand wrote an angry book in which she described the Mallorcans as 'thieves and monkeys'.

Valldemossa is also the birthplace of the island's patron saint, Santa Catalina Thomás, and nearly every house in the village has a painted tile beside the front door asking for the saint's protection.

THINGS TO SEE & DO

La Cartoixa (Charterhouse)

Visit the Charterhouse monastery to see the monk's cell where Chopin and Sand stayed, as well as the old pharmacy and an excellent museum of modern art including work by Picasso and Miró. There are regular recitals of Chopin's music and you can even buy a copy of Sand's book.
🕿 971 61 21 06 🕒 09.30–18.00 Mon–Sat, 10.00–13.00 Sun (summer), 09.30–16.30 Mon–Sat, 10.00–13.00 Sun (winter). Closed Sun (Jan & Feb)
🅸 Admission charge

> Don't leave Valldemossa without trying the local delicacies – *coca de patates* (light, fluffy buns dusted in icing sugar) – washed down with a chilled *ovxata d'ametlla* (almond milkshake).

SHOPPING

Valldemossa boasts plenty of small arts and handicraft shops, such as **Es Teix**, **Capamunta** and **Giravent**, selling fine handmade pottery, glass, jewellery, woodwork and table linen from all over the island.

Souvenirs Catalina Calafat This jam-packed shop sells everything from Lladró, lace and leatherware to *siurells* (clay whistles) and replica Chopin pianos. ⓐ Plaça Cartoixa 1, Valldemossa
ⓣ 971 61 24 61 ⓛ 10.00–19.00

Costa Nord

This cultural centre was established by Michael Douglas and Catherine Zeta-Jones. During the summer, it presents concerts in the evenings (see page 108). During the day, it offers an audio-visual show describing the history of the area.

ⓐ Avinguda Palma 6 ⓣ 971 61 24 25 ⓦ www.costanord.com
ⓛ 09.30–17.00

La Granja

One of Mallorca's finest country houses has been turned into a fascinating open-air museum of rural life and traditions. The best time to visit is during the 'folk fiesta' on Wednesday and Friday afternoons, when folk dancers perform in the courtyard and women in traditional costume give displays of lacemaking and embroidery. There are free tastings of various foods, and the restaurant serves up hearty portions of typical Mallorcan fare. The tour of the house includes the family chapel, the medieval kitchens, and a dungeon with a torture chamber!

ⓐ Carretera Esporles–Puigpunyent, Km 2, Esporles
ⓣ 971 61 00 32 ⓦ www.lagranja.net ⓛ 10.00–19.00 (summer), 10.00–18.00 (winter). Folk fiesta 15.30–17.00 Wed & Fri
ⓘ Admission charge

Lafiore Glass Factory

Glass has been made on the island since Roman times and glass-making techniques have changed little since then. Here, you can watch craftsmen at work in the glass-blowing workshop, before visiting the shop next door where jugs, vases, drinking glasses and candleholders are the most popular buys. They also sell reproductions of antique Roman glassware.

ⓐ Carretera de Valldemossa, Km 11, S'Esgleieta ☎ 971 61 18 00
ⓦ www.lafiore.com ◷ 08.00–20.00 ❶ Admission free

Port de Valldemossa

If you are brave enough to negotiate the 6-km (3¾-mile)-long helter-skelter drive that separates Valldemossa from its coastal port, you will enjoy numerous dramatic viewpoints and hair-raising hairpin bends

🔺 *Valldemossa has changed little over the years*

before entering the charming fishing village of Port de Valldemossa. Here you will discover a handful of stone cottages, a few fishing boats and a small stony beach – perfect for a light lunch and a swim, before setting off again up the corkscrew road.

TAKING A BREAK

Restaurants & bars

Es Port £ ❶ Set in Valldemossa's isolated fishing village, this small restaurant serves the freshest of fish and massive paellas. ⓐ Port de Valldemossa ❶ 971 61 61 94 ⓛ Restaurant 11.30–17.00, bar 10.00–17.00; closed early Dec–early Feb

Vesubio £ ❷ Traditional Italian restaurant with fresh pasta and homemade pizza dough. Star dish is *saltimbocca* (stuffed chicken breast). Extraordinary value. ⓐ Carrer Arxiduc Lluís Salvador 23, Valldemossa ❶ 971 61 25 84 ⓛ 13.00–16.00 & 20.00–23.00 Thur–Tues

Ca'n Costa ££ ❸ A handsome stone farmhouse on the road to Deià, this restaurant serves hearty Mallorcan specialities, including suckling pig, in a beautiful beamed dining room (originally the olive press). ⓐ Carretera Valldemossa–Deià Km 2.5 ❶ 971 61 22 63 ⓛ 12.30–16.00 & 19.00–23.30 Mon, Wed, Sun (Mar–Oct); 12.30–16.00 Mon, Wed, Thur, Sun, 19.00–23.00 Fri & Sat (Nov–Feb)

Ca'n Pedro ££ ❹ A large, atmospheric cellar restaurant on the edge of the village, serving hearty Mallorcan fare and homemade desserts. ⓐ Carrer Arxiduc Lluís Salvador ❶ 971 61 21 70 ⓛ 13.00–16.00 & 19.00–23.00; closed Sun night & Mon

Sa Cartoixa ££ ❺ *Tumbet* (Mallorcan ratatouille), rabbit stew, shoulder of lamb and paella are the specialities in this bustling café-restaurant, situated right at the heart of the village. ⓐ Plaça Ramón Llull 5 ❶ 971 61 60 59 ⓛ 08.00–23.00 Sun–Fri

Deià

The northwestern coastline between Andratx and Deià contains some of the most spectacular scenery on Mallorca, with pine-scented forests and terraced hillsides tumbling into the sea. This corner of Mallorca has long appealed to foreigners; Frédéric Chopin and Robert Graves were both drawn here, and Michael Douglas and Catherine Zeta-Jones as well as Richard Branson have homes in the area today.

Deià itself is a tiny village of ochre-coloured houses in the shadow of the Teix mountain. It was put on the map by the author and poet Robert Graves, who lived here from the 1930s until his death in 1985. His home is now open to the public, and he is buried beneath a simple, hand-inscribed tombstone outside the church of Sant Joan Bautista at the top of the village. Deià has become a magnet for foreign artists over the last few decades and the village is full of small art galleries and chic cafés. Having explored, you may wish to have a drink or a meal at the 5-star hotel La Residencia, which used to belong to Richard Branson.

THINGS TO SEE & DO

Ca N'Alluny

The beautiful stone house where Robert Graves lived from 1946 has been handsomely restored and opened to the public. The rooms are filled with his books and papers and a short film offers a potted biography of his life. Visits must be booked in advance.

ⓐ Carreterra de Sóller 1 ⓣ 971 63 61 85

ⓦ www.fundaciorobertgraves.com ⓛ 10.00–17.00 Tues–Sun

Cala de Deià

Just a 30-minute stroll from Deià, this tiny, pebbly cove with its jagged cliffs and icy, clear waters is one of the hidden gems of Mallorca's north coast. There is even a ramshackle beach bar and a restaurant, Sa Caleta (see page 81), for refreshments.

Museu Arqueológic de Deià (Deià Archaeological Museum)

A small but fascinating museum, worth visiting for the extremely
attractive conversion of an old mill. Prehistorical finds from nearby caves.
❸ Es Clot ❶ 971 63 90 01 ❺ 17.00–19.00 Tues, Thur and Sun
❶ Admission free

Son Marroig

This mansion was once the home of the wealthy Austrian aristocrat and
ecologist Archduke Lluís Salvador. He spent the best part of his life here
studying and recording Mallorcan wildlife and traditions. Today his
house is open to the public, providing a fascinating insight into island
life in the past. The garden houses a white-marble rotunda where he
sat and contemplated the sea and Sa Foradada, a rocky headland.
❸ Carretera Deià–Valldemossa ❺ 09.30–20.00 Mon–Sat (Apr–Sept);
09.30–18.00 Mon–Sat (Oct–Mar) ❶ Admission charge

TAKING A BREAK

Restaurants & cafés
Cafè Sa Fonda £ Once the village inn, this laid-back and welcoming café
is a local classic. On sultry summer nights, impromptu gigs take place on
the terrace. ❸ Via Arxiduc Lluís Salvador 3 ❶ 971 63 93 06
❺ 12.00–24.00 Tues–Sun; closed (Feb)

Pizzeria Las Palmeras £ Casual, friendly atmosphere. Serves snails, paella and squid, as well as pizza and pasta dishes, plus a wide selection of wines. Fabulous terrace, with great views of the village. ⓐ Carrer Arxiduc Lluís Salvador 11 ⓣ 971 63 90 16 ⓛ 13.00–16.00 & 20.00–22.30 Thur–Tues

Sa Caleta £ Grilled squid, prawns and swordfish are the specialities in this seaview restaurant, perched high on the cliffs over a picturesque cove. ⓐ Cala de Deià ⓣ 971 63 91 37 ⓛ 11.30–19.30, 12.00–18.00 & 20.00–22.00 Fri & Sat; closed Oct–Apr

Sa Font Fresca £ Family house turned into a classic, welcoming café offering a variety of tapas and sandwiches. ⓐ Carrer Arxiduc Lluís Salvador 36 ⓣ 971 63 94 41 ⓛ 07.00–22.30 Mon–Sat

Jaime ££ Elegant, contemporary Mallorcan cuisine served either on a lovely terrace, or in a rustic dining room. The desserts are heavenly. ⓐ Carrer Arxiduc Lluís Salvador 24 ⓣ 971 63 90 29 ⓛ 13.00–17.00 & 19.30–23.00 Tues–Sun

Miradors de Sa Foradada ££ This popular restaurant, clinging to a cliffside, specialises in Spanish and Mallorcan classics. ⓐ Carretera Valldemossa–Deià, Km 63 ⓣ 971 63 90 26 ⓛ 12.30–15.30 & 19.30–20.00 Fri–Wed

Ca'n Quet £££ Owned by the Es Molí Hotel, this restaurant enjoys an unforgettable setting, on a wooded hillside overlooking a stream. The fresh, modern Mediterranean cuisine is excellent. ⓐ Carretera Valldemossa–Deià ⓣ 971 63 91 96 ⓛ 12.00–15.30 & 19.00–22.30; closed Mon

Es Racó des Teix £££ If you splash out just once this holiday, consider doing it here at this Michelin-starred restaurant. The setting, the stunning views and the superb cuisine make it a very special treat. ⓐ Carrer Vinya Vella 6 ⓣ 971 63 95 01 ⓛ 13.00–15.00 & 20.00–23.00 Wed–Sun

Palma to Port de Sóller

The toytown train ride from Palma to Sóller is one of the highlights of any visit to Mallorca. The guards with their whistles, and the vintage carriages with their polished mahogany and brass panels, conjure up an image of a bygone age of travel. At the end of it all is a joyride down to the sea, in an antique tram imported from San Francisco.

The railway line, cut through the mountains in 1912, opened up Mallorca's previously inaccessible northern coastline to day-trippers

🔺 *Take the antique tram down to the sea*

from Palma. The tram service started the following year, and soon Port de Sóller became a fashionable resort. Nowadays the 'Mountain Express' is a must on every visitor's itinerary – with the result that the trains get very crowded at peak times. The best way to guarantee a seat on the train is to book ahead. Seven trains a day make the return journey from Palma, but, unless you are a keen photographer, you can escape the worst of the crowds by avoiding the 10.40 *turistico* train. The only advantage of this train is that it makes an extra stop at a scenic viewpoint overlooking Sóller.

More information is available at Ⓦ www.trendesóller.com

BEACHES

The two beaches at **Port de Sóller** are the only sandy ones along the entire northern coast until **Cala Sant Vicenç** (see page 40). The main beach runs beside the tramway. The second beach, **Platja d'en Repic**, fronts an attractive pedestrian promenade and is usually quieter. Both beaches have sunbeds, sunshades and pedaloes for hire, and there is also a windsurfing school.

THINGS TO SEE & DO

Boat trips
Some of the finest views of Port de Sóller and the Serra de Tramuntana mountains beyond can only be seen from the sea. Hop on a pleasure cruise from the port to Sa Calobra to see the spectacular **Torrent de Pareis**, Mallorca's Grand Canyon, where a narrow gorge empties into the sea across a shingle beach. Don't forget to take your camera.

Bunyola
The train rattles through the backstreets of Palma and out on to the plain, passing almond and orange groves before climbing to the hill village of Bunyola. If you want to break your journey, you can get off here to explore this pretty village and to visit the Tunel factory, where

many of Mallorca's herb-based liqueurs are made. Be sure to try the *palo*, a sweet, carob-based liqueur.

ⓐ Carrer Vinyetes, Bunyola

Mirador del Pujol d'en Banya

From Bunyola the train travels through a series of 13 tunnels; the longest one, Tunel Major, is just over 3 km (2 miles) long. There are three trains which stop at this *mirador* (panorama), leaving at 10.10, 10.50 and 12.15; you can enjoy a quick glimpse of the view over the Sóller valley as you pass. From here the train makes a curving descent towards Sóller, with the town appearing first to your left, and then to your right, as the track winds its way down the mountainside.

Port de Sóller

The Orange Express trams from Sóller to its port leave every 30 minutes from the station and the main square, passing through orchards of citrus fruit on their way down to the sea. Port de Sóller, with its wide sandy beach, makes an excellent place to stop for a couple of hours, wandering up to the lighthouse for scenic views of the port or enjoying a long lunch at one of the seafront restaurants. If you have time you can even take a boat cruise around the north coast from here.

THE WAY BACK

From Port de Sóller there are several options for the return journey. The last train to Palma leaves Sóller at 18.30 (19.00 in high summer) and to catch it you must take the 17.30 tram from the port. An alternative, if you feel like a change of scenery, is the bus journey to Palma, passing through the villages of Deià (page 79) and Valldemossa (page 75). There is also a faster bus route through the Sóller tunnel, which opened in 1997. Just think – if the tunnel had been there before, the railway would never have been built!

Sóller

The railway station at Sóller, based in a 17th-century manor house with overhanging jacaranda trees, is yet another throwback to the past and has two rooms of permanent displays, showing Miró paintings and Picasso ceramics. The town itself is well worth exploring (page 86) for a couple of hours.

TAKING A BREAK

Restaurants

Domenico £ Homemade pizzas, pasta and simply grilled fresh fish or meat are served in this friendly trattoria. There is plenty of choice for vegetarians, too. Finish up with the homemade tiramisú. ⓐ Carrer Marina 44 ⓣ 971 63 31 55 ⓛ 12.15–23.00 (June–Sept), 12.15–16.00 & 19.00–23.30 (Oct–May)

El Sólleric ££ International cooking, with a large terrace and private beach. You can even order from your sunbed by the sea! ⓐ Platja d'en Repic, Port de Sóller ⓣ 971 63 49 54 ⓛ 07.30–18.00 or 19.00 (depending on how busy it is)

Es Faro £££ Enjoy delicious fish dishes, served on a terrace high above the port affording exceptional coastal views. Leave room for a delectable homemade dessert. ⓐ Carretera Faro, Cap Gros de Muleta ⓣ 971 63 37 52 ⓛ 10.00–24.00 (Mar–Sept); 10.00–17.00 & 19.00–22.00 Mon & Wed–Sun (Oct–Mar)

AFTER DARK

Clubs

Altamar Discoteca The biggest and best disco in town, playing a variety of music to appeal to all ages. ⓐ Carrer Es Traves ⓣ 971 63 12 05 ⓛ 24.00–06.00 (mid-June–Sept), Fri and Sat nights only (Oct–mid-June)

Sóller

The friendly market town of Sóller (pronounced 'soy-air'), nestling in the lush Valley of Oranges at the heart of the Serra de Tramuntana mountains, never fails to captivate its many visitors. Its attractions include a cool climate with crisp mountain air, traditional lifestyle, and architectural interest as well as culinary delights.

THINGS TO SEE & DO

Alfàbia
The fountains work sporadically these days, but these gardens are lovely, green, cool and shady.
ⓐ Carretera Palma–Sóller (at the entrance to the Sóller tunnel)
ⓛ 09.30–18.30 Mon–Fri, 09.30–13.00 Sat (Apr–Oct); 09.30–17.30 Mon–Fri, 09.30–13.00 Sat (Nov–Apr) ❶ Admission charge

Biniaraix & Fornalutx
These tiny villages, nestled amid citrus groves in the foothills of the Serra de Tramuntana, are among the prettiest on the island. They are a pleasant stroll (30–60 minutes) from Sóller, and several excellent hiking trails can be found in the area.

Ca'n Det
This farm produces oranges and olives, extracting the oil in a press that dates from the 16th century. Buy some extra-virgin oil at the end of your visit. Visits by appointment.
ⓐ Ozona 8 ❶ 971 63 03 03

Lluc
The monastery at Lluc has been Mallorca's leading centre of pilgrimage ever since it was founded in the 13th century. It is connected with a miraculous statue of the Virgin. The story goes that a local shepherd boy discovered a dark wooden statue of the Virgin in a cave, where it had

been hidden during the Moorish occupation of Mallorca. A chapel was built to house the statue and now people come from all over Spain to pay homage to *La Moreneta* ('the little dark one').

There are also pleasant grounds for strolling and a Way of the Rosary designed by the famous Catalan architect Antoni Gaudí, and a museum. ☎ 971 87 15 25 ⓦ www.lluc.net 🕒 Museum 10.00–13.30 & 14.30–17.15 ① Admission charge 🕒 Basilica 08.00–20.00 ① Admission free

Museum Balear de Ciències Naturals (Natural History Museum)

This mansion once belonged to a wealthy merchant. Now the salons contain a collection of rocks and fossils, and displays explaining local botany. The highlight is the lovely Botanic Garden outside. ⓐ Carretera Palma–Port de Sóller, Km 30.5 ☎ 971 63 40 14 ⓦ www.jardibotanicsóller.org 🕒 10.00–18.00 Tues–Sat, 10.00–14.00 Sun ① Admission charge

⬥ *Lluc Monastery*

TAKING A BREAK

Restaurants & cafés

Bar Es Firó £ Bar-restaurant serving hearty country-style tapas. Try lamb with peppers and aubergines, fish in chilli or snails with wild mushrooms. ⓐ Plaça Constitució 10B ⏰ 08.00–22.00

Can Oliveret £ Rolls, cakes and pastries baked on the premises. Irresistible desserts. ⓐ Plaça Espanya 14 ☎ 971 63 45 09

Pastelería Ses Delicies £ Be sure to taste their mouthwatering plum cake and *pastisset de limone* (tarts made from local citrus fruits). ⓐ Plaça Constitució 12 ⏰ 10.00–19.00 Mon–Sat; closed Sun

Es Planet £ Soak up the sun and the atmosphere on the pavement terrace of this popular café in the main square. ⓐ Plaça Constitució 3 ☎ 971 63 45 70 ⏰ 07.00–22.00; closed Sun

Sa Cova ££ This restaurant on Sóller's main square serves international cuisine and Mallorcan specialities, such as rabbit with garlic. ⓐ Plaça Constitució 7 ☎ 971 63 32 22 ⏰ 13.00–16.00 & 19.30–23.00

El Guía ££ An old-fashioned restaurant which serves staple Mallorcan cuisine. The *menú del día* is always excellent value. ⓐ Carrer Castanyer 3 ☎ 971 63 02 27 ⏰ 13.00–15.00 & 20.00–22.00 Tues–Sat (summer); reduced hours (winter)

Luna 36 ££ Located in a former chocolate factory in the old town, this stylish café-bar and restaurant serves reasonably priced pizzas and salads, as well as fish and meat dishes. Eat out on the flower-filled terrace if you can. ⓐ Carrer de la Luna 36 ☎ 971 63 47 39 ⏰ 09.00–24.00 Mon–Sat

Ses Porxeres ££ Located inside a high-ceilinged barn beside the gardens of Alfàbia, this restaurant is renowned throughout the island for its

SHOPPING

The covered market on **Carrer Cristòfol Colom** sells fresh produce daily, and there is an open-air market in **Plaça del Mercat** on Saturdays 08.00–13.00.

Arteartesania sells contemporary jewellery, ceramics, and locally made wood and wrought-iron creations. ⓐ Carrer de sa Lluna 43 ⓣ 971 63 17 31 ⓦ www.arteartesania.com

Ben Calçat Small shoe-manufacturer specialising in traditional Balearic footwear. ⓐ Carrer de sa Lluna 74 ⓣ 971 63 28 74 ⓛ 09.00–13.00 & 16.00–20.00, closed Sat afternoons & Sun

Ca'n Oliver sells the distinctive Mallorca *roba de llengües* – cotton cloth with colourful stripy patterns, common in island homes. ⓐ Carrer de sa Lluna 25 ⓣ 971 63 82 05 ⓛ 09.15–13.30 & 17.00–20.00; closed Sat afternoons & Sun

Eugenio A treasure trove of Mallorcan pearls, fans and olive-wood souvenirs. ⓐ Carrer Jeroni Estades 11-A ⓣ 971 63 09 84 ⓛ 10.30–19.30 Mon–Fri, 10.30–18.30 Sat

game dishes. The wild boar and pheasant dishes are particularly recommended. ⓐ Carretera Palma–Sóller (at the entrance to the Sóller tunnel) ⓣ 971 61 37 62 ⓛ 13.30–15.30 & 20.30–23.00, closed Sun evenings & Mon; closed Aug

Bens d'Avalls £££ Very elegant, with fabulous views of the rocky coastline and the sea beneath. ⓐ Urb Costa Deià Ctra Sóller–Deià ⓣ 971 63 23 81 ⓛ 13.00–15.00 & 20.15–01.00 Tues–Sun, closed Nov–Apr

Sa Fàbrica de Gelats £££ This small ice-cream factory is well known for its creamy ices made from the valley's famous oranges and lemons. Choose from 25 varieties of ice creams. ⓐ Avenida C. Colom 13 ⓣ 971 63 17 08 ⓦ www.gelatsóller.com ⓛ 10.00–14.00 & 17.00–20.00

Pollença

Located between two hills, Pollença is the perfect Mallorcan town – a maze of narrow streets converging on a busy main square, where the traditions of café life and the siesta live on as if tourism had never been invented.

Don't miss the popular Sunday-morning market, when the main square, Plaça Major, is lined with fruit and vegetable stands, and artists set up their stalls in the backstreets behind the church. Buy a traditional Mallorcan basket and go shopping the Mallorcan way.

BEACHES

Regular buses leave from Pollença for the nearby beaches at **Port de Pollença** (page 43) and **Cala Sant Vicenç** (page 40).

🔺 *The steps leading to El Calvari*

THINGS TO SEE & DO

El Calvari (The Calvary)
A flight of 365 steps lined with tall cypress trees leads from the town centre to a small chapel with great views.

Pont Romà (Roman bridge)
This double-arched bridge across the dried-up riverbed of Torrent de Sant Jordi probably dates from the Roman occupation of the 1st century AD.

Puig de María (Mary's Mountain)
On the outskirts of Pollença, this hill is crowned by an old hermitage and defensive tower at its summit. Allow about an hour to walk to the top.

TAKING A BREAK

Cafés & bars
Bar Centro £ Situated between a church and Café Espanyol, here you will get a chance to meet the locals in a genuine and bustling tapas bar, set in the town's backstreets. ⓐ Carrer Temple 3 ⓣ 971 53 00 06 ⓛ 08.00–23.00; closed Wed

Bar Nou £ This popular locals' bar serves good-value, no-nonsense food at excellent prices. It's a great place to try the local *pa amb oli*. ⓐ Carrer Antoni Maura 13 ⓣ 971 53 00 05 ⓛ Restaurant 13.00–16.00 & 18.30–23.00, bar 11.00–24.00; closed Tues

La Birreria £ Young locals love this friendly bar, which boasts more than 50 types of beer from around the world. It also serves *pinxos* (French bread with different toppings) and light snacks including *pa amb oli*. There is a terrace on the main square in summer. ⓐ Carrer Colom 3 ⓣ 695 93 28 87 (mobile) ⓛ 19.00 until late Tues–Sun

⬤ *Enjoy Pollença's traditional café life*

Café Juma £ On the main square and part of a popular inn, this friendly café serves good tapas and light meals out on the terrace. ⓐ Plaça Major 9 ❶ 971 53 50 02 🕐 09.00–24.00; closed Dec

El Cantonet ££ The emphasis is on fresh homemade Italian food at this small, intimate restaurant in the backstreets of town. ⓐ Carrer Montision 20 ❶ 971 53 04 29 🕐 19.00–23.00; closed Tues and Nov–Jan

Il Giardino ££ Stylish Italian on the main square featuring sea bass in lemon sauce and steak in balsamic vinegar. ⓐ Plaça Major 11 ❶ 971 53 43 02 🕐 12.30–15.00 & 19.00–23.00; closed winter

Clivia £££ The speciality at this formal restaurant is seafood, brought daily from the port. The locals consider this one of the best restaurants in town. ⓐ Carrer Phillip Newman 3 ❶ 971 53 36 35 🕐 13.00–15.00 & 19.00–22.30; closed Mon and Wed lunchtimes (summer), all day Wed (winter)

Ca'n Costa £££ A chic restaurant housed in Pollença's first cinema, this serves excellent contemporary Mediterranean cuisine. Try wild game ravioli and chocolate torte. ⓐ Carrer Costa i Llobera 11 ❶ 971 53 12 76 🕐 19.00–23.00; closed Sun and winter

▶ *Discover Mallorca's unique culture*

Food & drink

Restaurants in Mallorca cater for a wide range of tastes – in the larger resorts you can get anything from an English breakfast to a Chinese take-away. Traditional Mallorcan cuisine, however, is typically Mediterranean, making full use of local products – especially pork, fish and vegetables – and heavily flavoured with garlic, tomato and herbs.

Popular Mallorcan dishes include *frit mallorqui*, a fry-up of liver, potatoes and tomatoes, and *sopes mallorquines*, a thick vegetable soup that contains slices of left-over brown bread, as well as the delicious *tumbet*, a ratatouille of potatoes, peppers and aubergines. The Mallorcans are hearty meat-eaters and charcoal grills are a speciality, along with roast suckling pig and shoulder of lamb. *Sobrassada* sausages, made by mincing raw pork with hot red peppers, can be seen hanging in butchers' shops and tapas bars, along with whole cured hams (*jamon serrano*). As for sea fare, lobster, prawns and sardines are always excellent, and sea bass baked in rock salt is a Mallorcan speciality.

PAELLA

The classic Spanish dish is paella, a mound of steaming rice flavoured with saffron and topped with everything from mussels and prawns to pieces of chicken. The Mallorcan equivalent is *arròs brut* ('dirty rice'), which uses chicken and pork but no seafood. Paella is available everywhere on Mallorca, but be wary of anyone who says they can serve it immediately – it takes at least 20 minutes to cook it properly.

TAPAS

These Spanish nibbles are designed to whet the appetite before a meal, but order enough of them and they can make a meal in themselves. They are usually lined up in a display cabinet along the bar in metal trays, so it is easy to pick out what you want. Typical tapas range from plates of ham, cheese and olives to more exotic offerings like fried squid rings, garlic snails, stuffed peppers and meatballs in tomato sauce.

● Sobrassada *sausages can be eaten hot or cold*

OTHER SNACKS

For a simple lunchtime snack try *pa amb oli*, an open sandwich which consists of thick brown bread rubbed with tomato and olive oil, and topped with ham or cheese. Another popular snack is *tortilla*, a potato omelette which is usually served cold with bread. Most bars serve *bocadillos* (filled rolls), and bakeries are a good place for stocking up on picnic provisions. Look out for *coca* (a kind of thin Mallorcan pizza), *empanadas* (small pasties filled with meat, fish or spinach) and *ensaïmadas* (spiral-shaped pastries that can be either savoury or sweet).

WINE & BEER

The *vino de la casa* (house wine) in most restaurants will probably be from Mallorca and is certainly worth a try. For something a bit more special, order a bottle of Rioja – these full-bodied, oak-aged wines come in both red and white varieties and are considered among the best in Spain. Cava, or Spanish champagne, makes an inexpensive treat and is sometimes combined with fruit juices for a refreshing cocktail. Beer (*cerveza*) is usually lager, sold either bottled or on draught – if you want draught, ask for *una caña*. Bars in the resorts have a wide selection of imported beers from Britain, Germany and elsewhere.

OTHER ALCOHOLIC DRINKS

Sherry (*fino*), served bone-dry and chilled, is the perfect drink to accompany a plate of ham before a meal. Another refreshing drink is sangría, an alcoholic fruit punch based on red wine, brandy and lemonade – delicious, but much more potent than it tastes. Most bars stock a good selection of Spanish brandies – popular brands include Soberano and Fundador – but for a truly local drink try *hierbas*, a herb-based Mallorcan liqueur which comes either sweet or dry.

SOFT DRINKS

The tap water is not always safe to drink in Mallorca, so most people prefer to drink mineral water – *agua con gas* is sparkling, *agua sin gas* is still. Popular drinks, such as Coca-Cola and lemonade, are available

● *Caught fresh from the Mediterranean, fish and seafood are always delicious*

TIPPING

Restaurant bills include a service charge but it is usual to leave an extra tip of around 5–10 per cent for good service. In bars, the custom is to leave your small change behind.

everywhere, and some bars offer freshly squeezed orange and lemon juice or *granizado*, which is a fruit drink with crushed ice. The Spanish always drink *café solo* after a meal – which is a small shot of strong, dark coffee, like an espresso – but visitors should have no trouble ordering other types of coffee such as *café con leche*, made with hot milk, or *descafeinado*, decaffeinated coffee. Tea (*té*) is also widely available in the resorts.

EATING OUT – A FEW TIPS

- The Spanish tend to eat very late. In most of the resorts it should be possible to get a meal at any time of day, but few restaurants in Palma open before 13.00 for lunch and 20.00 for dinner – and most people come a lot later than this.
- Many restaurants offer a *menú del día* at lunchtime – a set, three-course meal, often including wine or water, at a very good price. There is not always much choice but the food is always filling, local and fresh.
- Don't be afraid to try the local restaurants – almost all have English menus and even if they don't, the waiter will usually be able to explain what's on offer.

Menu decoder

Aceitunas aliñadas Marinated olives

Albóndigas en salsa Meatballs in (usually tomato) sauce

Albóndigas de pescado Fish cakes

Allioli Garlic-flavoured mayonnaise served as an accompaniment to just about anything – a rice dish, vegetables, shellfish – or as a dip for bread

Bistek or biftek Beef steak; *poco hecho* is rare, *regular* is medium and *muy hecho* is well done

Bocadillo Sandwich, usually made of French-style bread

Caldereta Stew based on fish or lamb. The Menorcan version with lobster is very popular

Caldo Soup or broth

Carne Meat; *carne de cerdo* is pork; *carne de cordero* is lamb; *carne picada* is minced meat and *carne de ternera* is beef

Chorizo Cured, dry red-coloured sausage made from chopped pork, paprika, spices, herbs and garlic

Churros Flour fritters cooked in spiral shapes in very hot fat and cut into strips, best dunked into hot chocolate

Cordero asado Roast lamb

flavoured with lemon and white wine

Embutidos charcuteria Pork meat preparations including *jamón* (ham), *chorizo* (see above), *salchichone* (sausages) and *morcilla* (black pudding)

Ensalada Salad – usually composed of lettuce, onion, tomato and olives

Ensalada mixta As above, but with extra ingredients, such as boiled egg, tuna fish or asparagus

Escabeche Sauce of fish, meat or vegetables cooked in wine and vinegar and left to go cold

Estofado de buey Beef stew, made with carrots and turnips, or with potatoes

Fiambre Any type of cold meat such as ham or *chorizo*

Flan Caramel custard, the national dessert of Spain

Fritura A fry-up, as in *fritura de pescado* – different kinds of fried fish

Gambas Prawns; *gambas a la plancha* are grilled, *gambas al ajillo* are fried with garlic and *gambas con gabardina* deep fried in batter

Gazpacho andaluz Cold soup (originally from Andalucia) made from tomatoes, cucumbers, peppers, bread, garlic and olive oil

Gazpacho manchego Hot dish made with meat (chicken or rabbit) and unleavened bread (not to be confused with *gazpacho andaluz*)

Habas con jamón Broad beans fried with diced ham (sometimes with chopped hard-boiled egg and parsley)

Helado Ice cream

Jamón Ham; *jamón serrano* and *jamón iberico* (far more expensive) are dry cured and *jamón de york* is cooked ham

Langostinos a la plancha Large prawns grilled and served with vinaigrette or *allioli*; *langostinos a la marinera* are cooked in white wine

Lenguado Sole, often served cooked with wine and mushrooms

Mariscos Shellfish

Menestra A dish of mixed vegetables cooked separately and combined before serving

Menú del día Set menu for the day at a fixed price; it may or may not include bread, wine and a dessert, but it doesn't usually include coffee

Paella Famous rice dish originally from Valencia but now made all over Spain; *paella valenciana* has chicken and rabbit, *paella de mariscos* is made with seafood and *paella mixta* combines meat and seafood

Pan Bread; *pan de molde* is sliced white bread; wholemeal bread is *pan integral*

Pincho moruno Pork kebab consisting of spicy chunks of pork on a skewer

Pisto Spanish version of ratatouille, made with tomato, peppers, onions, garlic, courgette and aubergines

Pollo al ajillo Chicken fried with garlic; *pollo a la cerveza* is cooked in beer and *pollo al chilindrón* is cooked with peppers, tomatoes and onions

Salpicón de mariscos Seafood salad

Sopa de ajo Delicious warming winter garlic soup thickened with bread, usually with a poached egg floating in it

Tarta helada Popular ice-cream cake served as dessert

Tortilla de patatas Classic omelette, also called *tortilla española*, made with potatoes that can be eaten hot or cold

Zarzuela de pescado y mariscos Stew made with white fish and shellfish in a tomato, wine and saffron stock

Mallorcan pottery is a beautiful souvenir

Shopping

GLASSWARE

You can watch glass being made at the **Lafiore glass factory** (see page 77) just outside Palma on the road to Valldemossa, or at **Ca'n Gordiola**, a glass-blowing workshop housed in a mock castle between Palma and Manacor. Many of the ornaments here come in striking blue and green designs.

LEATHER & SUEDE

Inca, in the island's centre, is Mallorca's third-largest town and is known as the 'leather town' because of the number of factories producing leather goods. Factory showrooms sell a wide range, from boots and shoes to handbags, jackets and belts. The quality varies and it pays to shop around – you will usually be offered a small discount if you buy in the factory shop, but you may find that prices are just as keen at a market or in the resorts. On Thursday mornings Inca is the setting for Mallorca's biggest traditional market, selling everything from fresh fruit to fine leather bags.

PEARLS

Majorica pearls come from a factory in Manacor – a few kilometres inland from Portocristo. You can visit it to watch the pearls being made and make purchases in their shops.

POTTERY

Rustic earthenware cooking pots make a good buy at country markets, together with *plats morenos*, glazed bowls painted with symbols of cockerels or flowers. A popular souvenir, especially for children, is a *siurell* – a clay whistle, painted white with splashes of red and green.

WOODCARVING

Sturdy bowls of carved olive wood make an excellent present – you can also find olive-wood ashtrays, coasters, eggcups and even earrings. **OlivArt**, a large factory shop at the entrance to Manacor from Palma, has the biggest selection of olive-wood souvenirs on the island.

Children

ANIMALS & ZOOS

Children always enjoy encounters with animals, and on the drive through the **Safari-Zoo** near Sa Coma (see page 53), they will get the chance to see zebra, giraffes, elephants and ostriches at close quarters. Take a tour of the zoo on the mini-train and they will enjoy it twice as much. Dolphins, sea lions and parrots perform acrobatics at **Marineland**, near Palma Nova (see page 25), where there are also sharks, monkeys and tropical birds on display. There are more parrots at **Jumaica** near Cales de Mallorca (see page 60) and more tropical fish at **Mallorca Aquárium** at Portocristo (see page 58). Best of all is Palma's brand-new aquarium in S'Arenal (see page 70), which opened in 2007.

MINI-GOLF

There are mini-golf courses in most of the resorts, but four of them have been developed into massive 54-hole complexes with enough other activities and attractions to occupy most of a day. These are **Golf Fantasia** at Palma Nova (see page 24) and at S'Arenal (see page 70), **Golf Paradis** at Sa Coma (see page 56) and **Super Golf**, part of the Hidropark water park at Port d'Alcúdia (see page 47).

WATER PARKS & THEME PARKS

In hot weather, children like nothing more than splashing about in the water, and if they tire of the beach you can always take them to one of Mallorca's water parks, where there will be enough pools, chutes and slides to keep them happy for hours. The biggest of all, with some thrilling rides, are **Aqualand** and **Western Park** next to it at S'Arenal (see page 70), and others are to be found at **Aqualand** in Magaluf (see page 27) and **Hidropark** in Port d'Alcúdia (see page 47). There is also a small water park attached to the wax museum at El Foro de Mallorca near Binissalem, on the Mallorcan Plains. Some of these can be visited on organised excursions, booked through your holiday representative, as well as independently.

The new **House of Katmandu** (see page 27) theme park in Magaluf will keep children of all ages entertained – the fantastical upside-down mansion offers a thrilling interactive adventure.

▲ *Aqualand is the biggest water park in Mallorca*

Sports & activities

ON THE GREENS

Many people come to Mallorca for the excellent golf facilities, with 18 excellent courses offering a variety of different challenges as well as some magnificent sea views. Most are situated close to the resorts. Shorts are allowed, but golfers are asked not to come in their beach gear.

Andratx Golf Club ⓐ Carrer M Cena 39, Camp de Mar ❶ 971 23 62 80 ⓦ www.golfdeandratx.com

Capdepera Golf Club ⓐ Roca Viva, near Cala Ratjada ❶ 971 81 85 00 ⓦ www.golfcapdepera.com

Club de Golf Son Servera ⓐ Near Cala Millor ❶ 971 84 00 96 ⓦ www.golfsonservera.com ❶ Nine holes

Club de Golf Alcanada ⓐ Port d'Alcúdia ❶ 971 54 95 60 ⓦ www.golf-alcanada.com

Golf Maioris ⓐ Llucmajor ❶ 971 74 83 15 ⓦ www.golfmaioris.es

Golf Pollença ⓐ Near Pollença ❶ 971 53 32 16 ⓦ www.golfpollensa.com ❶ Nine holes

Golf Poniente ⓐ Near Magaluf ❶ 971 13 01 48 ⓦ www.ponientegolf.com

Golf Son Gnal ⓐ Near Palma ❶ 971 60 38 51 ⓦ www.son-gnal.com

Real Golf de Bendinat ⓐ Near Illetes ❶ 971 40 52 00 ⓦ www.realgolfbendinat.com

Son Antem Golf Resort and Spa ⓐ Marriott Mallorca ❶ 971 12 92 00 ⓦ www.marriott.com/pmigs ❶ Two 18-hole courses

Son Muntaner & Son Quint ⓐ Carretera de Son Vida, Palma ❶ 971 78 30 03 ⓦ www.sonmuntanergolf.com

Son Termens Golf Club ⓐ Carretera de S'Esglaieta, Km 10 Bunyola ❶ 971 61 78 62 ⓦ www.golfsontermens.com

Vall d'Or Golf ⓐ S'Horta ❶ 971 83 70 01 ⓦ www.valldorgolf.com

WALKING & CYCLING

Mallorca offers plenty of opportunities for keen walkers and cyclists, from serious mountain challenges to flat coastal paths. The best hiking

🔺 *Windsurfing is very popular on Mallorca*

is to be found in the Serra de Tramuntana mountains along the north coast, but there are also plenty of good walks close to the resorts. Bicycles can be hired in most of the resorts and are a good way to explore the gentle countryside of the Mallorcan Plains. An easy, flat cycle path runs alongside the coast road between Alcúdia and Ca'n Picafort on Alcúdia Bay, enabling you to reach the S'Albufera nature reserve or to stop off at a lonely, dune-backed beach which cannot be reached by car.

IN THE WATER

Once you have got used to swimming in the sea, it does not take much extra effort to add a bit of snorkelling to the experience. Flippers and masks can be bought in a number of resort shops, allowing you to swim out into the crystal-clear water and peer down at the marine life beneath the surface. For a true underwater experience, you can learn to scuba dive. Most resorts have diving schools with trained professional instructors. These include **Centro de Buceo Zoea** at Santa Ponça (❶ 971 69 14 44 Ⓦ www.zoea.com), **Scuba Pollentia** at Port de Pollença (❶ 971 86 79 78) and **Michael's Diving School** at Cala d'Or (❶ 971 82 40 35). Remember that diving is only for experienced swimmers and that you should complete your last dive at least 24 hours before your flight home.

ON THE WATER

The calm waters around the Mallorcan coast provide ideal conditions for windsurfing and for sailing in dinghies and catamarans. Sailboards are available for hire at most of the major beaches, and sometimes tuition is available as well. Sailing boats can be hired from **Sail and Surf Pollença** at Port de Pollença (❶ 971 86 53 46) as well as at Cala d'Or and Font de Sa Cala near Cala Ratjada. Beginners will obviously need to stay close to the coast, but more experienced sailors can head off in search of remote beaches and deserted coves. For more high-octane thrills, sports such as waterskiing are available at some of the larger resorts – while if all you want is a gentle ride and a bit of exercise, you can hire out a pedalo or a canoe.

Festivals & events

CONCERTS

Classical music lovers should head for Pollença during the summer – the International Music Festival, held in the courtyard of a Dominican monastery between July and September each year, attracts leading musicians from all over Europe.

FESTIVALS

Mallorca's traditional festivals are some of the best places to meet the local people and experience the atmosphere of Mallorcan life. Every town and village celebrates its own saint's day, with street parties, music, dancing, fireworks, fancy-dress parades and general merriment. Many of the festivals are religious in origin, while others recall significant moments in Mallorcan history. Here is a summer guide to some of the most important events:

May

Moors and Christians Sóller is 'defended' against an 'invasion' of Moors in a stirring re-creation of Mallorcan history – usually on 8 and 10 May.

June

Midsummer's Night Known here as the Feast of St John, it is celebrated with fireworks, processions and beach parties across the island.

July

Fishermen's Festival A procession of fishing boats, this time in honour of the Virgin Mary, is held across Mallorca on 16 July. Portocristo has one of the best events.

August

Moors and Christians More 'battles' between historic enemies, this time in Pollença on 2 August.

Cavallets The famous annual festival of Felanitx, in which children dressed as hobby horses are chased through the streets by giants, takes place on 28 August.

September

Tourist Week Cala Ratjada lays on a week of festivities for visitors, including folk dancing, Spanish music and firework displays. Usually held in the last week.

FLAMENCO & FOLK DANCE

Flamenco is a gypsy folk dance which originated in southern Spain but is now performed all over the country, and you can experience flamenco and Mallorcan folk dancing in the evening at some resort hotels. For a really memorable evening, head for Son Amar (see page 21), Mallorca's top nightspot, where the all-star cabaret show (with dinner) features flamenco and Spanish dancing from the Carmen Mota ballet, who performed at the opening ceremony for the 1992 Barcelona Olympics. Tickets for this are usually booked up in advance, so it is best to arrange it through your resort representative. The Costa Nord cultural centre in Valldemossa hosts the summer music festival 'Noches Mediterráneas' which regularly features internationally famous flamenco singers and dancers. More info at Ⓦ www.costanord.com ❶ 902 25 03 33

> To find out what is happening in your area, ask at the local tourist office or pick up a free copy of *Where to go*, a newsletter published in English every three months. Concerts, plays and other events are also listed each day in the *Majorca Daily Bulletin*.
>
> Tourist offices also provide a leaflet for young people with lists of concerts and clubs, called *Mallorca Youthing*.

❶ *Mallorca is only a short flight away*

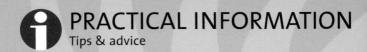

Accommodation

Price ratings are based on the average cost of a double room. These prices are rack rates. Look for deals on the Internet, which can bring official rates down by up to 70 per cent.

£	Budget	under 80 euros
££	Moderate	80–140 euros
£££	Expensive	140–200 euros

Hotel Born £ Fantastically located right in the centre, the city's best bargain is located in an elegant historic building. Rooms are simply but attractively furnished and the price includes a basic buffet breakfast. ⓐ Carrer Sant Jaume 3, Palma de Mallorca ❶ 971 71 29 42 ⓦ www.hotelborn.com

Hotel Sol Mastines Chihuahuas £ Reliable resort complex overlooking the bay with pools, bars, and entertainment for all the family. The rooms are basic but most enjoy splendid views over the cove. Half board is mandatory at peak periods. ⓐ Calas de Mallorca ❶ 971 83 33 01 ⓦ www.solmelia.com ❶ Closed winter

Hotel Marina Pax ££ Family friendly, with pools, kids' entertainment and a special children's buffet, the Marina Pax has a lot of repeat visitors. It's relatively quiet but still handy for Magaluf's famous nightlife. ⓐ Avinguda Notario Alemany 12, Magaluf ❶ 971 13 03 12 ⓦ www.marina-hotels.com ❶ Closed winter

Hostal Pollensa ££ Simple but stylish, this delightful little *hostal* is probably the best bargain in Pollença. It's located in a former inn, and some original touches have been kept to add character. The stylish rooms are all individually decorated. ⓐ Carrer Mercat 18, Pollença ❶ 971 53 52 81 ⓦ www.hostalpollensa.com

Meliá Cala d'Or Boutique Hotel ££ The rooms and suites are found in four buildings surrounded by lush tropical gardens. Facilities include three pools, including one for kids, gym, and sauna. ⓐ Carrer Portinatx 16–18, Cala d'Or ⓣ 971 64 81 81 ⓦ www.solmelia.com. ⓛ Closed winter

Protur Bonaire Aparthotel ££ A huge, well-equipped resort hotel set in gardens close to the beach, with pools, gym, sauna, bowling, and plenty of entertainment, especially for younger kids. The apartments are functional but good value. ⓐ Carretera Cala Bona-Costa los Pinos s/n, Cala Bona ⓣ 971 58 75 20 ⓦ www.protur-hotels.com ⓛ Closed winter

S'Hotel d'Es Puig ££ This hotel may be cheaper than the 5-star luxury hideaways for which this village is famous, but it remains tastefully stylish and characterful. The enclosed garden has a small pool. ⓐ Carrer Es Puig 4, Deià ⓣ 971 63 94 09 ⓦ www.hoteldespuig.com

Son Caliu Hotel Spa Oasis ££ Pamper yourself at this elegant and well-kept hotel, which is set in stunning tropical gardens. Spa facilities such as the sauna and Jacuzzi are free, but special treatments are also available. They also offer apartments. ⓐ Avinguda Son Caliu 8, Palma Nova ⓣ 971 68 22 00 ⓦ www.soncaliu.com

Cas Ferrer Nou Hotelet £££ A chic boutique hotel tucked away in Alcúdia's old quarter, this has just six individually decorated rooms. Prices are very reasonable and include wonderful breakfasts. There's a stunning roof terrace with loungers for you to soak up the sun. ⓐ Carrer Pou Nou 1, Alcúdia ⓣ 971 89 75 42 ⓦ www.nouhotelet.com

Esplendido Hotel £££ This historic hotel built in 1954 has recently been completely revamped into a modern-vintage seaside hotel and is now chic and fashionable. Most rooms have terraces offering spectacular sea views, and the beach is moments away. ⓐ Carrer Es Traves 5, Port de Sóller ⓣ 971 63 30 19 ⓦ www.esplendidohotel.com

Preparing to go

GETTING THERE

By air

Mallorca's airport is one of the busiest in Europe. It is well served by charter flights, and numerous standard and no-frills airlines operate services from airports around the UK. Prices are usually cheapest if you book well in advance. Many airlines charge a fee for telephone bookings, so book your flight online if possible.

Here are a few airlines:

British Airways W www.ba.com 📞 0870 850 9850

BMI Baby W www.bmibaby.com 📞 0871 224 0224

easyJet W www.easyjet.com 📞 0871 244 2366

FlyBe W www.flybe.com 📞 0871 522 6100

Iberia W www.iberia.com 📞 0870 609 0500

Jet2 W www.jet2.com 📞 0871 226 1737

Monarch W www.flymonarch.com 📞 0870 040 5040

Thomas Cook W www.thomascook.com 📞 0870 750 5711

Thomsonfly W www.thomsonfly.com 📞 0870 1900 737

Many people are aware that air travel emits CO_2, which contributes to climate change. You may be interested in the possibility of lessening the environmental impact of your flight through the charity Climate Care, which offsets your CO_2 by funding environmental projects around the world. Visit w www.climatecare.org

By sea

Regular car ferries link Mallorca with Barcelona (journey time 7 hours, or 3 hours 45 mins in the fast catamaran) and Valencia (8 hours, or 4 hours 30 mins in the catamaran) on the Spanish mainland. There are also several services a day to the Balearic islands of Ibiza and Menorca.

Balearia W www.balearia.com 📞 (+34) 902 160 180

Transmediterranean W www.transmediterranean.com 📞 (+34) 902 454 645

Package holidays

The cheapest way to get to Mallorca is to book a package holiday with one of the leading tour operators specialising in Spanish holidays. The best deals are available online though, and it is always worth shopping around, especially if you can be flexible with your dates. Here are a few tour operators:

Airtours Ⓦ www.airtours.co.uk ☏ 0870 238 7788

Bargain Holidays Ⓦ www.bargainholidays.com ☏ 0871 230 0653

Direct Line Ⓦ www.directline-holidays.co.uk ☏ 0870 300 8 300

easyJet Holidays Ⓦ www.holidays.easyjet.com ☏ 0871 244 2366

First Choice Ⓦ www.firstchoice.co.uk ☏ 0871 200 7799

Holiday.co.uk Ⓦ www.holiday.co.uk ☏ 0870 040 2400

Thomas Cook Ⓦ www.thomascook.com ☏ 0870 750 5711

Thomson Ⓦ www.thomson.co.uk ☏ 0870 165 0079

TOURISM AUTHORITY

The Spanish tourist authority (Turespaña) has offices throughout the world, including the UK. These are all listed on the official Spanish tourist information website, Ⓦ www.spain.info, which provides a good introduction to the country. For specifically Mallorcan information, have a look at Ⓦ www.infomallorca.net (from the Mallorcan Tourist Board) and Ⓦ www.illesbalears.es (run by the Balearic government). Both are excellent resources and are available in several languages including English. The city council in Palma de Mallorca has also produced a useful website in English Ⓦ www.palmademallorca.es

Spanish Tourist Office UK ⓐ 79 New Cavendish Street, 2nd floor, London W1W 6XB ☏ 0207 486 8077 Ⓦ www.tourspain.co.uk

BEFORE YOU LEAVE

Reciprocal agreements are in place which allow EU citizens to claim free health care within EU member countries. You will need an EHIC (European Health Insurance Card), which can be ordered in the UK from the website Ⓦ www.ehic.org.uk, by calling ☏ 0845 606 2030, or by collecting an application form from post offices.

It is not necessary to have inoculations to travel in Europe, but you should make sure you and your family are up to date with the basics, such as tetanus. It is a good idea to pack a small first-aid kit to carry with you containing plasters, antiseptic cream, travel sickness pills, insect repellent and/or bite relief cream, antihistamine tablets, upset stomach remedies and painkillers. Sun lotion can be more expensive in Mallorca than in the UK so it is worth taking a good selection, especially of the higher factor lotions if you are taking children with you, and don't forget after-sun cream as well. If you are taking prescription medicines, ensure that you take enough for the duration of your visit – you may find it impossible to obtain the same medicines in Mallorca. It is also worth having a dental check-up before you go.

ENTRY FORMALITIES

Citizens from the United Kingdom and the Republic of Ireland must show a valid passport when entering Spain. Visitors from other EU countries need a valid passport or national identity card. Visitors from Canada, the USA, Australia and New Zealand (among other countries) need a valid passport and may remain in Spain for a maximum period of 90 days without a visa. Citizens of most other countries, including South Africa, must apply for a visa at the nearest embassy or consulate before travelling to Spain. These regulations are subject to change and you should always check with the Spanish authorities before travel.

EU residents may carry any quantity of tobacco goods and alcohol which can be deemed to be for 'personal use' when travelling within the EU. Visitors to Spain from non-EU countries (if over 18) may bring 200 cigarettes, or 100 cheroots, or 50 cigars, or 250 grams of rolling tobacco, plus one litre of drink (over 22 per cent alcohol by volume), or two litres (under 22 per cent alcohol by volume). Perfumes are limited to 50 grams of perfume and 0.25 litres of eau de toilette.

MONEY

The currency in Spain is the euro (€), which is divided into *centimos*. Euro bills are available in denominations of 500, 200, 100, 50, 20, 10 and 5, and the coins come in denominations of 50, 20, 10, 5, 2 and 1 *centimos*. Each country mints its own coins with a different 'heads' side but a common 'tails'. Therefore you could easily find yourself making your purchase with French or Italian coins and receiving change in Greek or German coins!

The easiest way to access cash in Mallorca is to withdraw it from a cashpoint (*telebanco*) using your card and PIN. Commission taken by your bank varies, but it is usually between 2 and 3 per cent. All but the very smallest villages will have at least one cashpoint. There are bureaux de change at the airport and in the larger towns and resorts, but banks usually give a better deal. Credit cards are usually accepted in larger hotels, restaurants and shops but are rarely accepted in smaller establishments. When paying by credit card, you must show your passport or valid ID.

CLIMATE

Mallorca enjoys a temperate Mediterranean climate. The hottest months are July and August, when temperatures regularly reach 30 °C (86 °F) or more, but the weather is generally warm and sunny from May to September. Winters are mild, except on high ground, and temperatures rarely drop below 10 °C (50 °F). The rainiest months are October and November. The weather can be very changeable in winter and spring, so pack a rain jacket and umbrella.

The best time to come depends on what kind of holiday you are looking for. For a great beach holiday with plenty of nightlife, come in July and August, but accept that there will be crowds and queues for everything. June and September are still warm but the island is not as crowded. In spring (April and May), the countryside is at its most verdant and this is the best time to come for a walking holiday. The winter months are popular with older holiday-makers who enjoy the peace and quiet and the mild temperatures.

BAGGAGE ALLOWANCE

Most airlines have a baggage weight allowance of 20 kg for checked luggage. Some airlines, particularly the no-frills airlines and charter airlines, restrict luggage weight to 15 kg.

During your stay

AIRPORTS

Mallorca's airport, Son Sant Joan, is 11 km (7 miles) southeast of Palma de Mallorca. It is a large airport with all the amenities, including car rental offices, bureaux de change, cash machines and tourist information booths. These can all be found in the arrivals hall. The taxi stand is just outside (€15–20 to get to the town centre). A public bus (no 1) leaves approximately every 15 minutes for Palma.

COMMUNICATIONS

Public phones

Public telephones can be found easily in all the major towns and resorts. Most accept both coins and telephone cards (available from tobacconists). Put the coin in the slot and then push in the metal button on the side to make it drop.

TELEPHONING MALLORCA FROM ABROAD

Dial the international access code (00), 34 (Spain country code) then the nine-digit number.

TELEPHONING ABROAD

Telephoning **Australia** 00 + 61 + area code (minus the 0) + telephone number

Telephoning **New Zealand** 00 + 64 + area code (minus the 0) + telephone number

Telephoning the **Republic of Ireland** 00 + 353 + area code (minus the 0) + telephone number

Telephoning **South Africa** 00 + 27 + area code (minus the 0) + telephone number

Telephoning the **UK** 00 + 44 + area code (minus the 0) + telephone number

Telephoning the **United States** and **Canada** 00 + 1 + area code (minus the 0) + telephone number

> ## BEACH ETIQUETTE
> Topless bathing is acceptable on most Mallorcan beaches, though nudity is only officially permitted at **Es Trenc** on the south coast and **Platja Mago** near Magaluf. While attitudes have relaxed about wearing beachwear off the beach, tourists should dress more appropriately in resorts and towns, especially Palma itself.

Spain is one of the most expensive European countries as far as telecommunications are concerned, so if you are going to call abroad, it is a good idea to buy an international phone card from a *locutorio* or *estanco*, or call from a *locutorio*.

Post
Visitors are recommended to use only the official yellow post boxes when posting mail or postcards, as boxes operated by private companies are not proving to be very reliable. Stamps are also available from any *tabac* (tobacconist).

Internet
If you need to check your email, you can do so at one of the many internet cafés. Nowadays, many hotels will also offer this facility, as may bigger *locutorios*.

CUSTOMS
Mallorcans have their own language called Mallorquí and a culture and history which is quite distinct from much of the rest of Spain. Paella, flamenco and sangría, for example, are not part of Mallorcan culture. Locals are very grateful when visitors acknowledge their cultural difference, perhaps simply by saying 'bon dia' (good day in Mallorquí).

DRESS CODES
In Mallorca, beachwear – swimsuits, shorts, etc. – are worn on the beach and not elsewhere. Most locals make an effort to dress up for the

EMERGENCIES

For all emergencies (police, fire, ambulance and coastguard), dial 112.

In a medical emergency, go to the nearest health centre (look in the phone book under *Centres de Salud*) and remember to take your European Health Insurance Card. The main hospital in Palma is the **Hospital General, Plaça Hospital** ❶ 971 21 20 00.

If you are robbed, see **HEALTH, SAFETY & CRIME** (page 120).

British Consulate The consulate is there to give advice and replace lost passports, but staff will not become involved in any holiday/hotel problems which are the province of the hotel/tour operator. They can give advice on transferring money and provide a list of lawyers, English-speaking doctors, dentists, etc. ❸ Convent dels Caputxins no 4, Edificio Orsiba B, 4th D, Palma ❶ 971 71 24 45 ❿ www.britishembassy.gov.uk ❸ 08.00–15.30 Mon–Fri

evening stroll and to dine out in restaurants. However, they recognise that most holiday-makers, particularly if they are travelling with children, have come to relax and won't be dressing up. If you are visiting any churches, however, particularly the cathedral in Palma, ensure that you are dressed suitably (no shorts or strappy tops) or you may be refused entrance.

ELECTRICITY

Electricity is supplied at 220–225 volts. Spanish plugs are of the two-pin round-plug variety so an adapter will be required for British and non-Continental appliances. If you are considering buying electrical appliances to take home, always check that they will work in the UK before you buy.

GETTING AROUND
Car hire

There is plenty of choice of car hire companies. Drivers should be over 21 and have held a driving licence for one year. Fully comprehensive insurance is advisable. Seat belts are compulsory in the front seats and, where fitted, in the back seats. Children under 12 must sit in the back.

Driving

Drive on the right. The speed limits in force are 120 km/h (75 mph) on motorways, 100 km/h (63 mph) on dual carriageways and 90 km/h (55 mph) on single carriageways except in urban areas where it is 50 km/h (32 mph). The Guardia Civil, the police in green uniforms, patrol the highways, issue fines and carry out breathalyser tests. These are very strict, with limits of 0.5 g per litre or 0.3 g per litre for drivers who have held a licence for less than two years.

If you meet a coach on a narrow, twisting, mountain road, going up or down, you are the one who must reverse. There are few public phones on motorways if you do have a breakdown. There is an extensive network of petrol stations on the island. Some are self-service, many stay open 24 hours and all accept credit cards. Note, however, that no change is given between 21.00 and 08.00.

There are several underground car parks in Palma and several more in the pipeline. The ones by the cathedral and under the Plaça Major are undoubtedly the most popular, so be prepared to queue. Palma and many other towns operate restricted parking areas, known as ORA. Tickets can be obtained from nearby machines and should be displayed inside the windscreen. There is a discount on parking and speeding fines if they are paid promptly at the nearest town hall or the bank listed on the ticket.

Public transport

The bus service is good, but buses do get very crowded in summer. Routes are available from the tourist information offices. The driver is paid on boarding, so try and have small change ready.

The old wooden train which links Palma with Sóller is a must on any tourist itinerary, although it is quite expensive. It connects with an equally old wooden tram which takes passengers to Port de Sóller. There are also very inexpensive local trains from Palma to Inca, where the line divides, with one branch extending to Manacor via Sineu, and the other to Sa Pobla via Muro.

Taxis are white. All taxis are obliged to post fares in the interior of the car. A small supplement applies for each piece of luggage in the boot, for trips to or from the airport, and after 22.00 and at weekends. Check the fare before setting off, and always ask for a receipt. If you feel you have been overcharged, ask for a receipt so that you can make an official complaint at the Dirección General de Consumo (equivalent to the UK Consumers Ombudsman ⓐ Carrer Sant Gaietà 3, Palma ① 971 17 62 62).

Beach trains
Several resorts have beach trains that run alongside the sea and are a delightful way of travelling to your favourite spot on the beach.

Horse-drawn carriages
Galeras are an alternative choice for sightseeing in Palma. There are ranks beside the cathedral and the Passeig de Sagrera, with a list of fares.

HEALTH, SAFETY & CRIME
The biggest health hazard in Mallorca is excessive exposure to the sun, which can result in sunburn, dehydration and, in extreme cases, sunstroke. Avoid the sun between 12.00 and 16.00, wear a good sun protection lotion and take particular care with children. Drink plenty of water to stay hydrated. The tap water is not always safe to drink but bottled water is easily available from supermarkets.

A change of diet may cause tummy upsets, but remedies are easily available from local pharmacies.

Mosquitoes can be a problem at the beginning and end of summer. Cover up, wear mosquito repellent, and use a plug-in device in your hotel room (readily available in Mallorca) to keep them at bay.

All Mallorcan towns and resorts have a public health centre (*centres de salud*). Show your EHIC when you arrive.

For minor ailments, go to a pharmacy (*farmacia*), where the highly qualified pharmacists can recommend remedies. Pharmacies are

In hot climates, it is important to use a strong sunblock

easily recognised by their flashing green sign. They take it in turns to open outside usual shop opening hours, and a list (look for '*farmacia de guardia*') is posted in the window of every pharmacy.

Mallorca is relatively safe. There is little major crime, but petty theft and bag snatching is unfortunately common. Keep all valuables in the hotel safe, ensure doors and windows (particularly if there are balconies) are locked. Keep photocopies of all official documents (passport, traveller's cheques, travel insurance). Avoid the gypsy flower sellers at all costs. They are persistent and skilful thieves. In the main resorts, you may be hassled by touts selling timeshares. It's best to ignore them completely.

If you are robbed, you must make a police report (*denuncia* in Spanish). You can make this report by telephone (☏ 092). You will still have to go to a local police station (*Comisaría de Policía*) to sign the report, but doing a phone report first will save you hours of waiting.

In the towns and resorts, you will probably deal with the local police (in blue uniforms). The Guardia Civil are largely responsible for road safety.

MEDIA

British daily newspapers are widely available from newsagents and outdoor *kioscos* found in every town and resort. The wonderful English-language newspaper *Majorca Daily Bulletin* provides wide coverage of local events and English sport. The tourist information office offers a free quarterly publication entitled *Where to Go*, supplemented by a weekly agenda called *Mallorca Week*. These publications are also available in PDF format from Ⓦ www.infomallorca.net. For live music and club nights, pick up *Mallorca Youthing*, a free leaflet found in tourist offices and venues around the island.

Most mid-range and top-range hotels offer cable or satellite TV stations, and every resort will have several pubs with TV screens for catching up on your favourite soaps, or watching major sporting events.

OPENING HOURS

Shops are usually open from 9.00 or 10.00 until 13.30 or 14.00, and from 16.00 or 17.00 until 20.00 or 21.00. Large shops, supermarkets, hypermarkets and most chains do not close at lunchtimes. Smaller shops, particularly in the smaller towns, close on Saturday afternoons. All shops, except in resorts, close on Sundays. In the resorts, shops open every day and stay open later in season but may close altogether in winter.

Banks are usually open 08.30–14.30 Monday to Friday and closed on Saturdays. Hours may differ in tourist resorts. Cash machines usually operate 24 hours a day, 7 days a week.

The main post office in Palma is at Plaça Constitució 6 🛈 971 22 86 10 🕓 08.30–22.00 Mon–Fri, 09.30–22.00 Sat, 12.00–22.00 Sun. Smaller post offices in other towns and villages usually close at 14.30 and don't open on Sundays.

Each town and village has a big weekly market that is always worth a visit, whether you are looking for local fresh food or souvenirs. The tourist information offices can provide a complete list. Among the biggest are the following: Alcúdia and Artá (Tuesday), Port de Pollença (Wednesday), Inca (Thursday), Sóller and Palma (Saturday), and Pollença and Santa María del Camí (Sunday).

RELIGION

Spain is a Roman Catholic country and visitors are most welcome to attend Mass in local churches. High Mass is celebrated in Palma Cathedral on Sundays and public holidays at 10.30. The Anglican Church is also present. ❷ Carrer de Nunyez Balboa 6, Palma ❶ 971 73 72 79 ◷ Sunday service is at 11.00

TIME DIFFERENCES

Mallorca is one hour ahead of GMT. As in the UK, clocks go forward one hour on the last Sunday in March and go back one hour on the last Sunday in October. Add or subtract the given number of hours to or from Spanish time to get the time in each country.

Australia +8 hours
New Zealand +10 hours
United Kingdom +1 hour
US Eastern Time −6 hours
US Pacific Time −9 hours

TIPPING

Locals rarely tip, but there are different expectations of tourists. Tip between 5 and 10 per cent in taxis and restaurants and perhaps a couple of coins in bars and cafés if you are pleased with the service.

TOILETS

While there are public toilets on most of the main beaches, they may not be particularly clean. Many bars and restaurants now post signs stating that the toilets (*serveis* in Mallorquí or *servicios* in Castillian Spanish) are only for customers, so you may be expected to buy something if you want to use the bathrooms. Facilities in fast-food restaurants and department stores are always good standbys.

TRAVELLERS WITH DISABILITIES

Facilities for disabled travellers have improved dramatically in recent years but there is still a long way to go. Modern hotels, restaurants, museums and galleries are required to provide wheelchair access. Most of the public bus network is now wheelchair-accessible and there are special taxis available for disabled visitors (for more details see Ⓦ www.cruzroja.es).

The Calvià Council provides sea bathing chairs free of charge on its beaches at Palma Nova, Magaluf, Santa Ponça, Peguera (Torà beach) and Ses Illetes (🄣 971 13 91 39). For information on activities contact **Aspayn** (🄣 971 77 03 09) or **Asprom** (🄣 971 28 90 52).

The Tourism Board has recently published a fantastic new resource which offers a comprehensive list of all facilities for disabled visitors on the island. This is available to download from Ⓦ www.infomallorca.net and is called *Mallorca per Tothom* (*Mallorca for Everyone*). It is published in several languages, including English.

WEIGHTS & MEASURES

Spain uses the metric system of kilos and grams, but you can always buy two or three apples or half a dozen bananas, for instance. When shopping, you will find that most articles of clothing show British and European sizes.

Petrol is sold in litres and you can ask for a full tank (*lleno*) or *diez* (10) euros or *veinte* (20) euros. Distances are in kilometres and metres.

Imperial to metric	Metric to imperial
1 inch = 2.54 centimetres	1 centimetre = 0.4 inches
1 foot = 30 centimetres	1 metre = 3 feet, 3 inches
1 mile = 1.6 kilometres	1 kilometre = 0.6 miles
1 ounce = 28 grams	1 gram = 0.04 ounces
1 pound = 454 grams	1 kilogram = 2.2 pounds
1 pint = 0.6 litres	1 litre = 1.8 pints
1 gallon = 4.6 litres	

ACKNOWLEDGEMENTS

We would like to thank all the photographers, picture libraries and organisations for the loan of the photographs reproduced in this book, to whom copyright in the photograph belongs:

D. Ashmore (pages 9, 103)
FLICKR (S. Chaudry page 10; B. Seravalli pages 1, 23; A. Blight page 24; J. Best page 33; L. Cervis page 53; A. Smith page 77; M. Riddlesworth page 90; G. Ruiz Mitjavila page 95; D. Danzig page 96; W. Winkler page 100; S. Pixel page 109)
Pictures Colour Library Ltd (page 121)
Thomas Cook Tour Operations Ltd (pages 5, 13, 18, 41, 50, 57, 59, 61, 67, 73, 82, 87, 91, 93, 105)

Project editor: Diane Teillol
Layout: Donna Pedley
Copy editor: Anne McGregor
Proofreader: Jan McCann
Indexer: Marie Lorimer

Send your thoughts to
books@thomascook.com

- Found a beach bar, peaceful stretch of sand or must-see sight that we don't feature?

- Like to tip us off about any information that needs a little updating?

- Want to tell us what you love about this handy little guidebook and more importantly how we can make it even handier?

Then here's your chance to tell all! Send us ideas, discoveries and recommendations today and then look out for your valuable input in the next edition of this title.

Email to the above address or write to:
HotSpots Series Editor, Thomas Cook Publishing, PO Box 227, Unit 9, Coningsby Road, Peterborough PE3 8SB, UK.